THE SALES PROFESSIONAL'S SURVIVAL GUIDE

THE SALES PROFESSIONAL'S SURVIVAL GUIDE

A Blueprint for Tactical Prospecting

MIKE LaRusso

BOOKLOGIX®
Alpharetta, GA

The information contained within this book is strictly for educational purposes. If you wish to apply the ideas contained in this book, you are taking full responsibility for your actions. Some examples and details, including products and industries mentioned in this book, may have been changed. Although the author and publisher have made every effort to ensure that the information in this book was correct at the time of first publication, the author and publisher do not assume and hereby disclaim any liability to any party for any loss, damage, or disruption caused by errors or omissions, whether such errors or omissions result from negligence, accident, or any other cause.

ISBN: 978-1-6653-0200-5 - Paperback
eISBN: 978-1-6653-0201-2 - eBook

These ISBNs are the property of BookLogix for the express purpose of sales and distribution of this title. The content of this book is the property of the copyright holder only. BookLogix does not hold any ownership of the content of this book and is not liable in any way for the materials contained within. The views and opinions expressed in this book are the property of the Author/Copyright holder, and do not necessarily reflect those of BookLogix.

Library of Congress Control Number: 2023903125

Printed in the United States of America   0 9 1 9 2 3

⊗This paper meets the requirements of ANSI/NISO Z39.48-1992 (Permanence of Paper)

*I dedicate this book to all the Sales Professionals
who must overcome endless prospecting obstacles.*

CONTENTS

PREFACE

The ability to acquire new business is the most sought-after reward in sales. In the past, this ability was simply accepted as a common trait of a Sales Professional, and the more naturally talented they were at business development, the more they produced. But functional inadequacies exist within an organization that impedes the hunt for new business opportunities. And when Management ignores the true origin of these impediments, they attribute the failure to supposed inadequacies within the Sales Professionals themselves. Therefore, to "correct" this misconception, Management creates extensive processes that hamper sales and are controlled by people with no direct relation to the organization's sales functions, nor to their negative results.

I was interviewed by a sales trainer for a consulting position with a company that had outsourced their sales functions to the trainer and his organization. My responsibilities would be to prospect for new customers. The sales trainer informed me that the company instituted strict sales practices, which he'd learned from about a dozen sales training books. He mentioned the titles and asked if I had read any of them. I told him, "No."

He seemed disappointed, then continued by describing his mandatory sales activities. The salespeople had to come into the office every morning by 8:00 a.m. regardless of the location of their sales territory. They were required to update the Customer Relationship Management database with their planned activity for the day, then travel to their territory to prospect by knocking on at least fifty doors. Then they had to return to the office by 5:00 p.m. At the office, they would have to update the Customer Relationship Management database with the results of their activity and enter the planned activity for the following day. Every

Tuesday morning, there would be one hour of general sales training, one hour of roleplaying, and every Thursday there would be a four-hour telemarketing session. You were required to meet with twenty prospects a month, and finally, you would be required to have five lunch or dinner meetings with prospects per month. I was about to ask how that metric would be tracked, but he volunteered that information.

"We review your monthly expense reports to track entertainment spending." I said it sounded like those steps would use up a lot of my prospecting time.

He replied, "It's all about activity! Now, let's talk about you. You were recommended to me as having a superior ability to generate new business. How do you go about your daily prospecting?"

At this point, I didn't believe he would accept my methodology, so I just confidently responded with the results of my prospecting methods. "I will commit to doubling the company's sales quota in the first ninety days, or I'll resign." He seemed to be unequipped to respond to my directness, and remained silent for several seconds.

He replied, in a seemingly canned response, "Let's get down to brass tacks. How many cold calls did you make yesterday?"

I said, "None."

In a surprised tone, he asked, "Why not?"

I replied, "Because I had four closing appointments."

Concerned with the lack of cold calling, he stated, "That's no good. That's not enough activity."

I replied, "But I closed three out of the four deals."

He forcefully replied, "That's results, that's not activity!"

It was obvious he didn't believe the sales metrics I had claimed, probably because he'd never seen that level of production before. It was at that point I realized that the sales profession had morphed into a tool used to implement mandatory processes, essentially, to justify another's existence in the organization. I would have turned down the position, but it was never offered to me.

New business acquisition has been removed as a normal part of sales talent and has become an activity categorized separately from other sales activities. As new business development has been isolated to a type of selling, so has the Sales Professional engaging in the activity. They have been identified by a title and a responsibility. They're labeled as the company's "hunter," or business development manager. So, if a Sales Professional is assigned that singular role, then what is the rest of the sales force doing to generate new business?

Well, those poor people are the ones found sitting in a sales-training classroom, being force-fed prospecting methods that differ in name but are infected with a sameness of technique. Consequently, the Sales Professionals who don't possess an innate talent to acquire new business are left to squeeze out what success they can from these antiquated prospecting methods. Methods which are designed as monuments to effort but are, in fact, relics to results.

In my many consulting positions, I have observed and experienced a multitude of sales happenings. I've used these events as the foundation for a documented framework of business-development tactics that I've implemented through my intuition and my wits. The result is a structured manual and reference guide. *The Sales Professional's Survival Guide: A Blueprint for Tactical Prospecting* explores the origin and presence of prospecting hurdles faced by Sales Professionals. And I provide an in-depth tutorial on the Tactical Prospecting Methodology and the Alliance Process. I believe that the processes learned here will incentivize the creation of newer methods of productivity and will succeed in making natural-born salespeople out of trained ones.

INTRODUCTION

You're Making Money on My Time

At some point in your sales career, you may miss quota, be put on a performance-improvement plan, get laid off, or lose your job because your company went belly-up or got bought out. Perhaps your specific industry will change in some manner and your ability to prospect for new business will stagnate. Maybe you'll be uncertain as to why your sales situation and career are continually precarious. And all that time, you will work your tail off, obediently following the marching orders of others who control every aspect of your prospecting activity but who won't suffer a single consequence if you fail. So, I'll assume you have a genuine interest in learning new prospecting methods to avoid this or you're desperate for any alternative.

Well, there is an alternative. I will reveal prospecting techniques, some of which you may have considered but have refrained from exploring because you couldn't make them work, you didn't know how to start, or your attempts had no support from Management. You may also be distrustful of new methods because your previous experience and training were nothing more than a collection of hollow catchphrases that offered painfully obvious advice parading as revolutionary.

Why won't my methods also be painfully obvious? As a consultant, my responsibilities could include conducting sales analyses, negotiating partnerships, or hunting for new business. I typically worked on a six-month contract and had to create methods that rapidly produced results. But more importantly, there is nothing that has infuriated me more as a Sales Professional than having been required to engage in prospecting activities that grew muscles for Management but had no chance of producing results for myself. If I voluntarily chose a prospecting method that ultimately proved to be fruitless, then that was on me, and I learned from it and moved on. But it was constantly on my mind that I was being forced to engage in unproductive activity, again and again, while postponing my own productive methods, stealing my time to pay for someone else's time. It didn't matter if that other person was a sales trainer, a manager, or the supervisor that hired me. At that point, the only thing that mattered was that my livelihood was tied to my production, and my production was tied to required and minimally successful prospecting methods. Therefore, the reason my methods are now different is that I can't afford to promote unproductive prospecting techniques that only appear to be revolutionary. You can't afford to spend your time learning them either.

A VP of sales was reciting a tale of a salesperson who drove by ABC Company every morning and proclaimed that, one day, he was going to sell them his product and nothing was going to stand in his way. The salesperson called, and knocked, and emailed, and tried all the typical methods to communicate. Then finally, after four years, he broke through, got an appointment, and, by the fifth year, ultimately made the sale. Success!

We were all supposed to be inspired to do the same through perseverance. That may sound like an inspiring story, but for one thing, I can assure you that during the five-year process, the salesperson either closed other sales or had a rich spouse to sustain him while waiting for that specific one. And I can also assure you that those other self-sustaining sales were not prospected in the same manner. But that's all okay, so long as you devote only the same percentage of time equal to the method's success rate. If 1 percent of your prospecting time is devoted to the "whale," and after five years of selling other customers, you succeed in selling the "whale," that's also okay. What isn't okay is trying to portray singular perseverance as the sole technique for chasing all prospects. There is no way that VP would do the same thing in the same situation. Never! But he'd spend five years telling you to. And how many hundreds of other salespeople drove by that same company, proclaiming the same thing, and didn't accomplish anything other than a PIP or termination letter from their supervisor? No sales story ever ends without supporting the storyteller's method.

Part of the unspoken truth is that Management is searching for any newer prospecting methods and doesn't know how to adjust the existing ones to better accommodate a new sales environment. But unfortunately, I don't think it would matter if they did. The change wouldn't be worth the risk to them. Sales has become the only part of an organization in which high turnover is blamed on the victims and is accepted by the supervisors as a normal, almost-necessary consequence of employing Sales Professionals. If the prospecting methods are continual and unchanging, then poor results will also be. And if Management has complete faith in their prospecting techniques, then they'll think the poor results must be attributed to the Sales Professional's incompetence, and punishments will ensue. Even when I've experienced incomprehensible turnover rates of various sales teams, the mandates are continual, as are the resulting failures.

You may become exasperated, distressed, and believe you're at fault over your apparent failure to produce, I'm here to tell you that you aren't. How can I be so sure? Because it's in a Sales Professional's makeup to close business and to do deals, regardless of the product. And that can't be done if it becomes virtually impossible to get in front of a customer. And to me, "impossible" is defined as the minimal prospecting success rate at gaining an appointment that exists with common prospecting methods. A "one out of a hundred" appointment success rate is much closer to zero successes than it is to actual successes. And a lot of successes are what's needed for a lot of success.

I will show you that extremely productive prospecting techniques do exist, and they are based in Tactical Prospecting. I'm sure if you look around your sales world and see that not all Sales Professionals are suffering in the same manner. Some may even be producing tremendous results month after month while others sit wondering what they're doing differently. If you analyze the life cycle of their prospects, you'll soon realize they have been derived from some form of Tactical Prospecting, even if by accident.

And it doesn't matter whether they're aware of it; they would never admit it even if they were. Management seems to prefer gaining appointments through extensive activity, while accomplishing the same objective through minimal effort is frowned upon. "Work smarter, not harder" is what's proclaimed, but the opposite is what's expected. Not here! Our goal is to gain appointments in the least amount of time, regardless of the effort. This will be accomplished by learning the tenets of Tactical Prospecting as the foundation needed to institute the Alliance Process.

The sales environment has dramatically changed, but prospecting strategies have remained stagnant. My methods won't be like the prospecting trainings you may have experienced, because now you're making money on my time. I have an *obligation* to provide you with something of value—and that is what I intend to do.

Throughout the text, I use some familiar terms and some newly created ones. But each has its own definition as it relates to the Alliance Process and my experiences. I frequently refer to the terms Management and Sales Professionals as the two entities that have distinct effects on sales. A Sales Professional is defined as any individual in any role who's responsible for generating sales revenue for an organization. Management is an inclusive term representing any entity that can institute a level of control over those individuals and their sales activity. This control can be exerted by direct supervision or indirect control through the enforcement of procedures. Management can be any person in any area of the business at any level. Regardless, if this individual is a rank-and-file member, an outside agent, a member of operations, or is in a true supervisory position, the only distinguishing characteristic of Management, for the purposes of this text, is that they can control a Sales Professional's time. I use these labels to conceptualize two types of individuals in an organization: one who is engaged in revenue-generating behavior and another who can obstruct that behavior either by design or by accident.

PART ONE

The Tactical Mentality

THE TACTICAL MENTALITY begins with a new way of thinking about sales. This mentality must saturate the entire staff of an organization. Every department, every function, and every individual must believe and behave with the goal of closing sales as the motivation for everything they do. This does not mean that a level of oversight or practical control of these functions should be forfeited; it simply means processes must be developed with the benefit of sales foremost in their creation. This also applies to individuals whose responsibilities consist of supporting sales and also to alternative sales functions that are indirectly connected to making the sale. With a unified focus on the sale by all members of an organization, the expertise of each can be directed toward this end, according to their specialized abilities. The result is a collection of divergent methods achieving convergent results. For instance, if a sales support worker's responsibilities are involved with legal contract review, and they maintain the same conviction toward making the sale as the Sales Professional, then their expertise with contract negotiation can be directed toward maintaining the structure of the contract without threatening the deal by stubbornly defending minuscule details. The spirit of the contract terms can be maintained while the agreement benefits both parties.

I was the VP of Sales in an industry with a product that had become very commoditized. To increase sales, I identified a market demand for an expensive version of the main product and isolated that customer segment. Since these items were so valuable, upper management removed them from the main inventory department and they were placed under the control of the accounting department. This would ensure their security and allow for meticulous recording of the inventory. I promoted a strategy, and the increased earnings potential to the sales force by focusing their sales effort on this new market. Since the competition for this product was fierce, it required that orders be filled within one day of the sale. The resulting orders for this product skyrocketed. However, over time, the supervisor in the accounting department became intolerant of the daily interruptions stemming from sales' requests for the product. A restrictive schedule was put into place by accounting, reducing the time orders could be placed from daily to merely two days a week and two hours per day. Since the sales force could not fill orders quickly enough, the sales for this product fell to zero. Ultimately, I convinced upper management to put the inventory department under my supervision, and I instilled an understanding of the needs of the sales force into an operations function. The sales for the specialized product increased beyond the previous levels and, as an unexpected benefit, the company became a market leader in sales for the commoditized product as well.

As it relates to the prospecting process, Sales Professionals must align their thinking, beliefs, and activity solely with the end goal of making the sale as the first step in hunting for new business. This may seem contradictory to a typical selling process, which contains steps leading to the goal. If that's the case, good! Preliminary prospecting objectives (such as gaining an initial meeting) cannot take the place of what you're truly going after—the customer's spending income. When weaker initial objectives are the focus—such as establishing communication with a prospect or gaining the appointment itself—greater effort is applied to a less powerful outcome, and the prospecting process is artificially lengthened.

The Focal Points of the Tactical Mentality

1. DEFINE the characteristics of the ultimate, most-valuable goal for the organization, which in this case is making the sale.

2. FOCUS solely on that end goal during every aspect of the prospecting process from beginning to end. Do not focus on intermediary objectives. Focusing on the sale from the outset fosters thinking and identification of direct routes to the true end goal. It also encourages the creation of methods to overcome experiential obstacles, directly obstructing the end goal, that are encountered as a normal result of engaging in competitive business activities.

3. NAVIGATE the most-direct route to the goal by developing business practices that identify and immediately capitalize on Opportunities that assist in reaching that specific goal.

Artificial Steppingstones

One of the most important tactical advantages of a unified focus is the prevention of disruptive strategies that highlight less-meaningful achievements along the prospecting route and give them inflated importance. For instance, if sales are not achieved quickly or frequently enough to assess a Sales Professional's performance, Management will identify numerous intermediary accomplishments leading up to the sale, such as a number of lunches with a client or a number of proofs of concept. They then erroneously correlate the number of lunch meetings to be the cause of the sale rather than the effect of the customer's interest in buying. These ancillary activities are then made mandatory steps, supposedly necessary to close sales. More lunches create more sales, according to Management. Ultimately, the extraneous steps become the new goals, separate from the true end goal of a sale. For example, if a certain number of appointments per week is the focal point, then gaining an appointment becomes the initial goal, creating extra selling steps and consequently extra points of delay. To illustrate, if we view a common selling process taught by sales trainers, we can see how this occurs:

Typical Sales Process Steps to Reach a Goal

The steps focused on making a sale:

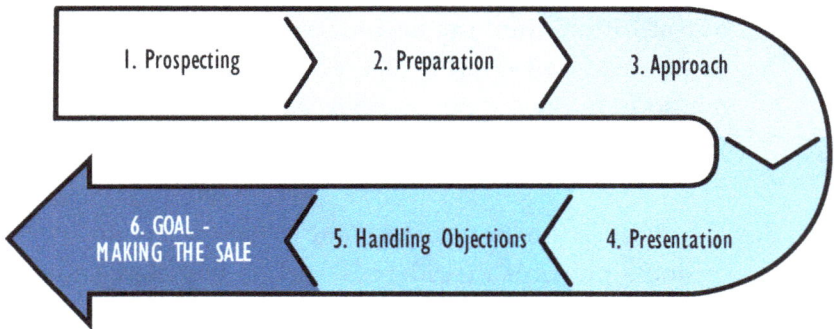

```
1. Prospecting  >  2. Preparation  >  3. Approach

6. GOAL -        <  5. Handling Objections  <  4. Presentation
MAKING THE SALE
```

Each step will focus the thinking and behavior on the end goal of the sale:

1. Prospecting for the perfect matching customer with a need for your product.
2. Preparing the presentation to satisfy the customer's requirements needed to make a purchase.
3. Approaching the decision-maker with the ability to make the purchase.
4. Presenting the offering with the requirements needed for the customer to purchase.
5. Handling and overcoming any objections and obstacles blocking the sale.
6. Making the sale and offering the follow-up activity to ensure satisfaction.

However, when the new intermediary goal is gaining an appointment, the process' steps are still present, but focused on requirements needed to gain an appointment:

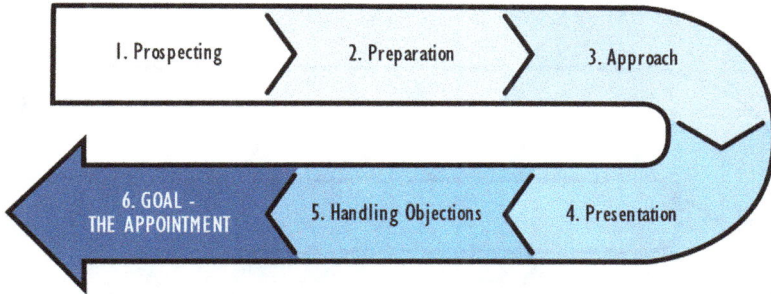

1. Prospecting	2. Preparation	3. Approach

6. GOAL - THE APPOINTMENT	5. Handling Objections	4. Presentation

And when these steps are addressed and successfully satisfied, it still doesn't produce a sale; it produces only an appointment.

Now, if another intermediary goal is assigned to the process, such as gaining a demo presentation, this creates a second phase of process steps that relate to the new goal. The different requirements associated with these steps are addressed and overcome.

These steps are focused on gaining a demonstration.

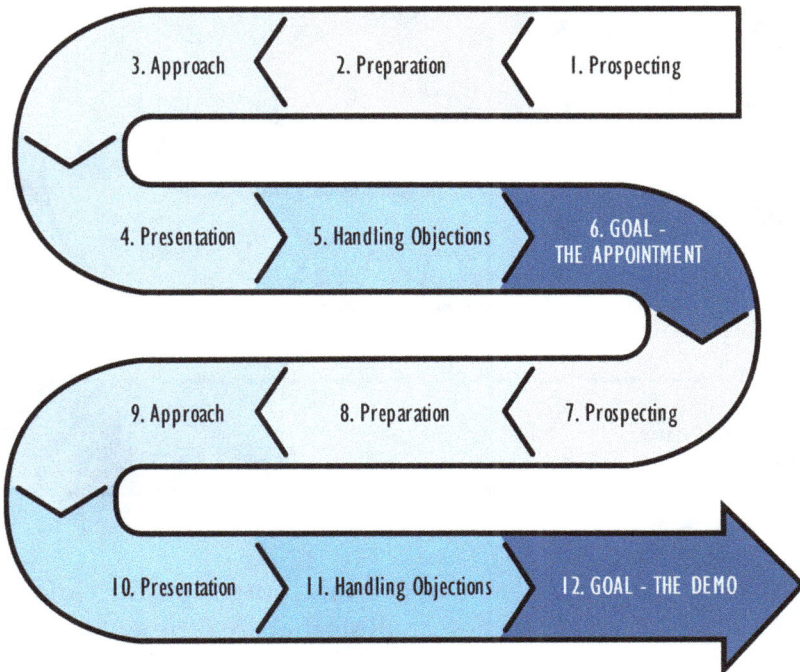

3. Approach	2. Preparation	1. Prospecting

4. Presentation	5. Handling Objections	6. GOAL - THE APPOINTMENT

9. Approach	8. Preparation	7. Prospecting

10. Presentation	11. Handling Objections	12. GOAL - THE DEMO

Until the final, true goal of making a sale is pursued, it creates a third phase of process steps that need to be addressed and overcome. The final steps focus on the issues associated with closing the sale:

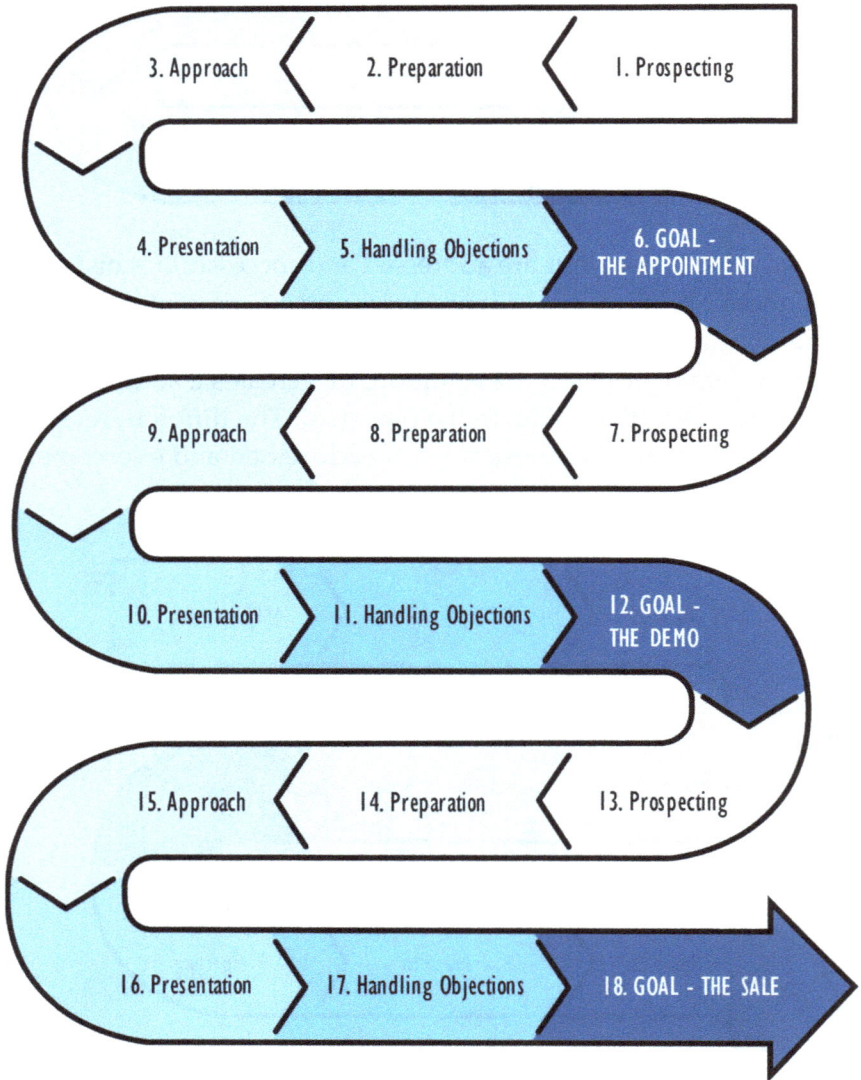

3. Approach	2. Preparation	1. Prospecting
4. Presentation	5. Handling Objections	6. GOAL - THE APPOINTMENT
9. Approach	8. Preparation	7. Prospecting
10. Presentation	11. Handling Objections	12. GOAL - THE DEMO
15. Approach	14. Preparation	13. Prospecting
16. Presentation	17. Handling Objections	18. GOAL - THE SALE

The process steps encountered while pursuing the various goals will require research and analysis that are different in each phase, depending on the characteristics of each separate goal. For instance, prospecting to achieve a demo appointment may require less-stringent matching characteristics of the customer type, so the population of potential customers may be larger but less targeted. Or the decision-maker with the authority to accept a demo could be different from the one who approves the purchase of a product. And certainly, the presentations for a proof of concept will differ widely from a closing appointment presentation. With different goals, there are different requirements associated with the same basic steps. With the pursuit of more and more unnecessary intermediary goals, more process obstacles are created. Eventually, the route to the true goal of making the sale becomes a mile long.

These typical sales process steps are generic and are used merely to illustrate my point of accumulating points of delay as a function of the chosen end goal. In general, there are always selling steps that must be addressed and satisfied between the start and end of any typical prospecting cycle, but they vary according to the end goal. The key difference with the Tactical Mentality is that when the goal at the beginning of the prospecting process is making a sale, then a series of strategic encounters directed toward making the sale are employed as soon as prospecting begins. This greatly reduces any delays and unsuccessful attempts at meeting with a potential customer. There are fewer prospects available to gain a demo presentation than to just gain an appointment, and there are even fewer available to make a sale. Therefore, when the focus at the beginning and throughout the prospecting process is on making the sale, randomization is eliminated.

To be clear, however, the Alliance Process is built upon Tactical Prospecting and its principles. It does not incorporate any of the selling processes or steps similar to what has been described here. As will be shown, with Tactical Prospecting, the common sales process steps are eliminated. And with the Alliance Process, not only are common points of delay avoided but also the quality of the prospect and the time saved on making the sale are infinitely superior, as shown below.

Path Expedited with the Alliance Process

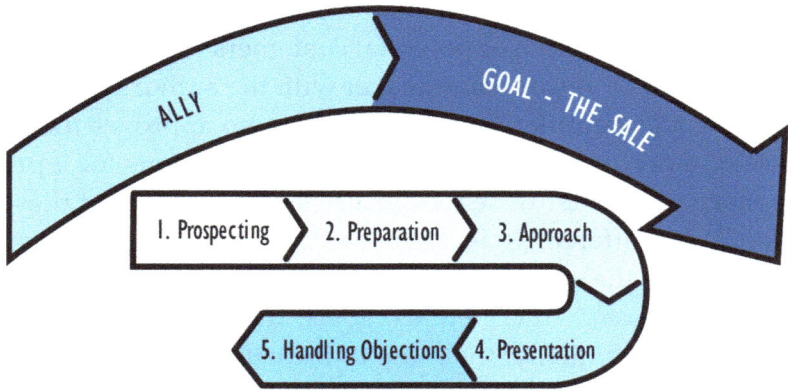

A unified focus removes any need to engage in precursor steps as some type of feedback mechanism for Management. Gaining the sale is the first thought when prospecting, and the appointment is the residue of that design. Rather than wasting time trying to convert intermediary objectives in order to create interest, the Tactical Mentality envisions and engages in activities that directly achieve the ultimate goal at the outset. This will accomplish Tactical Prospecting's intent, which is to identify interested prospects, not create them.

CHAPTER 1

Real Productivity

TO ENGAGE IN REAL PRODUCTIVITY, you must understand what productivity really is. Productivity is tangible, concrete results. It is derived from focusing on what ultimately needs to be attained and by building the most-direct route to it. Productivity is getting to that destination with the fewest steps possible and is achieved with both a creative and a formal process of tactical engagements that each constitutes some type of accomplishment. It can be pointed to and identified as the catalyst for the next step of a profitable gain. That catalyst can be anything from information to making initial contact to any form of **Significant Interaction** that created a tangible reward. And, of course, that includes the final reward of a sale. If the goal of making a sale can be

> **Significant Interaction:** a communication with the purpose of business development in the form of identifying, engaging, or negotiating Opportunities.

achieved in a single step, or a single day, or with your feet up on the desk with apparent ease, you've still achieved your goal.

To be productive, the universal end goal must be the main, initial focus of your effort, not a singular selling objective that may have been assigned to you. I'll say it again: *the universal end goal, the ultimate result, must be the focal point, regardless of any preliminary objectives.* Productivity is not the level of effort expended, the raw number of individual attempts, or some measure of resulting euphoria felt by Management after witnessing your endless activity. There's no honor simply in incessant, isolated effort. "Not gaining anything" is not an accomplishment just because it is one less attempt that can be crossed off a tally list, reducing the total effort by some arbitrary number. And if, by chance, you do attain the goal in one single success or happen to achieve the same goal after a thousand failures, the process is completely meaningless if you have no idea what caused the difference. And the luck of the draw is not a reason.

I was in a meeting at which Management was attempting to justify continual, random prospecting activity. A supervisor created the phrase "Right Place, Right Time, Right Opportunity." In other words, if you keep making random, cold introductions attempting to gain an appointment, it will eventually happen. And the key word in that description is you. *If* you *keep doing it. Not* him. *I'm not including those supervisors who venture out of the office one day out of the year, walking around your territory just to get a free aerobics workout, and then bragging for the next 364 days about their willingness to cold call. The irony was that this supervisor finished every rah-rah speech with his own prospecting dictum: "Hope is not a strategy." Like, I hope that I hit quota. But that's exactly what his philosophy was based on: hope. Like, I hope I run into a stranger that has the need and the ability to buy my product. It's true, hope isn't a strategy, but neither is coincidence.*

The most tyrannical system of all is if you *do* know which tactic created the difference between your successes and failures, but are not permitted to concentrate solely on that successful tactic. Real productivity is achieving steady results from a knowledgeable control of your own process. You cannot depend on a process that includes a strategy based on the law of averages, because if your outcome is random, then so is your income.

Don't Worry

I won't leave you stranded in the sales desert with no more than a basic idea or catchphrase, as you're probably used to. I will provide you with deep explanations, steps, methods, and the measurement tools to confirm the productivity levels of your activities quickly and efficiently.

Real Measurement

The Monthly Prospecting Production Equation

There are an overwhelming number of grossly misinterpreted sales metrics, mainly because the data is never viewed with a logical application to the selling results. They are values used as propaganda supporting conscripted sales labor. The prospecting values are mnemonically recited, such as "one hundred doors a day," by Management, sometimes for years without reviewing or accepting any contradictory metrics. What they see is what has always been. If they viewed that data without bias, by merely breaking down the numbers into a simple application, it would be apparent that whatever methods are required aren't working, or whatever goals are linked to those methods are unattainable.

One of the measurement tools I created that is designed to operate within the boundaries of a realistic scenario is the Monthly Prospecting Production Equation. This equation is used to determine an accurate level of production within each individual sales environment if I were to follow the selling mandates required by that individual organization. This tool has also proved extremely useful in initial meetings with potential consulting clients because I can determine right out of the gate whether the consulting position I am considering is a winning proposition.

I was interviewing for a sales consulting position to sell in an industry in which I had absolutely no previous knowledge or experience. The products could cost tens of thousands of dollars so I assumed it had a lengthy sales cycle that could affect my earnings potential in the first year. The salary was much lower than average because there was an expected above-average commission earnings.

I asked the sales manager what I could expect to earn in the first year. She directed me to a whiteboard that listed the sales team's individual commissions for the previous month. She pointed to the top producer who had earned $196,000 in commissions for the month! I was not naïve and understood there must be some unknown factors providing that sales-person an advantage, especially since the next closest producer had earned one-tenth that amount. However, my initial impulse was naïve when I calculated that if I could earn just 3 percent of that amount, I'd be fine for the first year. A Sales Professional should never think in those terms because the proportional differences in commission levels are never equally proportional to the differences in the selling requirements. The differences are drastic.

To resolve this uncertainty, I created an equation to calculate the commission earnings potential using the data from a specific selling environment. The sales manager was very accommodating and allowed me to ask any questions I liked about the position. So, I did. I asked twelve key sales metric questions related to the industry and the company, such as average sales cycle and average revenue per sale. Once I input that data into my equation, which I have on my phone, I was able to determine that the true commission earnings potential was about $1,000 per month. A figure that was nothing close to what was being promoted. I didn't give my discovery to the sales manager, I simply asked, "Why does the top producer do so well?"

She responded, "He works harder cold calling," which, of course, wasn't the reason. So, my next move was obvious. I negotiated an annual commission guarantee that would provide enough income for me until I could figure out what advantages the top producer had, which would take me less than a year.

The power of this equation lies in its immediacy. The resulting calculation can instantly convert an industry novice into an industry veteran by providing true production measurements that others in the organization probably don't even know, including Management. This is accomplished by using the sales metrics that are supplied by **Management**, the enforcers of the mandates. It prevents any basis for disagreement or debate. **Management** is simply telling you what is occurring in their business, and you're saying *okay*. Then here's what a **Sales Professional** can produce according to the data provided.

> **Sales Professional:** any entity that is responsible for generating sales revenue.
>
> **Management:** any entity, at any level, that can control any amount of a sales professional's time.

Monthly Prospecting Production Equation Factors

Starting with a month's worth of prospecting time, or 173 hours:

First, determine the total amount of prospecting time available by adding up non-prospecting activity time:

1. How many set appointments are there in a month, and how long is each appointment session?

2. How many training sessions are required per month, and how long is each session?

3. How much administrative time is required to do paperwork, CRM input, or other administration?

4. How much commuting and travel time is involved for the required locations?

5. How much time is used servicing a customer after the sale?

6. What is the average time for an existing account appointment?

7. What is the average time for a new account appointment?

Next, determine the total amount of time required to gain an appointment using the required methods:

8. What is the hourly investment of time to gain one appointment?

Then, determine the percentage of appointments that will close a sale:

9. What is the closing ratio for a new account?

10. What is the closing ratio for an existing account?

Finally, determine the average dollar volume of a sale and the length of the sales cycle:

11. What is the average dollar revenue generated per sale?

12. What is the average sales cycle length for New Appointments and Existing Appointments?

The Components of the Equation

TPH	Total Available Prospecting Hours
NPH	Non-Prospecting Hours
NCSApptH	New Customer Set Appointment Hours
AveV	Average Customer Visits to Completion
NCSAppt	New Customer Set Appointments
ECSAppt	Existing Customer Set Appointments
ECSApptH	Existing Customer Set Appointment Hours
HPAppt	Hourly Prospecting Time per Appointment
NCCR	New Customer Appointment Closing Rate
ECCR	Existing Customer Appointment Closing Rate
ARS	Average Revenue per Sale
MSC	Monthly Sales Cycle

I can almost guarantee that Management will not have an answer to some of the necessary parameters, so use experience as a guide. Also, for some of the available parameters, the data will be horribly skewed toward belief and away from reality. But that's also okay, because an unrealistically successful hourly investment of time per appointment, or an extremely high closing ratio, will be reflected in superior results in the equation. However, those stated results would then be confirmed in the actual sales numbers generated by their present salesforce. And if the two didn't match, then Management would be forced to alter the data they provided, as well as their bogus self-promotion. Reality would prevail.

In addition to validating these results with the actual sales numbers produced, consider qualifying those results with further questioning. The two main questions then would be (1) how many of the salespeople are hitting quota, and (2) what is the sales rep turnover? If the first is low and the second is high, you'll know that you've been misled. Hard truth would prevail again.

The data gained from these simple questions will be more than enough to determine what a Sales Professional will earn in a certain selling environment—if you were to do exactly what you're told by Management. The equation looks like this:

Monthly Prospecting Production =

After viewing this measurement tool, you may feel overwhelmed. Worse, you may decide to take the easy route back to familiar prospecting methods. Stay with me. I've introduced the Monthly Prospecting Productivity Equation to whet your appetite and offer a sample of the accurate measurement tools created for the Sales Professional. As we proceed through the upcoming sections, I will reveal and explain in-depth the repertoire of equations and analysis procedures used in Tactical Prospecting.

Work Smarter Not ~~Harder~~ Martyr

We are going to dispose of the oft-commended, but totally use-less, incessant activity for the sake of activity and of Management. We're going to learn how to work smarter for the real reward: the sale. Tactical Prospecting is designed to greatly reduce the time invested in gaining appointments with a superior closing ratio. The thought process of Tactical Prospecting is taking ownership from beginning to end of prospecting activity and improving, altering, or discarding the behavior according to specific objectives. These objectives include creating a success—whatever that is as defined by you—in the shortest time possible, keeping genuine measurement of the prospecting behavior as a feedback tool, and identifying people who can best assist with reaching a **Target**. This is the foundation of pure hunting.

> **Target:** an entity that can provide any level of prospecting productivity.
>
> **Opportunity:** the availability to establish the quickest agreed-upon relationship with a person who has access to your Target.

First, I'll start with a warning. Tactical Prospecting may appear to be suspiciously like that thing called "networking." Well, on the surface, it might be defined in the same manner, but it shouldn't. The activities that have been described and performed by Sales Professionals labeled as "networking" have become characterized to mean any activity that isn't labeled cold calling. In fact, this kind of activity is even worse than cold calling. With cold calling, at least you're randomly reaching out to different **Opportunities**, so there is an increasing chance of success. Although painfully low, the potential is still there. But the behavior labeled "networking," usually at planned events, consists of interacting with a lot of the same people repeatedly, hoping they have changed their minds about agreeing to an appointment since your last interaction. And they're hoping the same about you. Secondly, when networking is performed properly, it is a very manual, labor-intensive process. Therefore, any prospecting activity that is not considered cold calling is called networking, and the resulting failures are also associated with the term. Because the behavior of engaging face to face has become so unlearned in a prospecting environment, it is no longer taught to Sales Professionals because no one knows how to teach it. For these reasons, I am forced to refrain from using the term because when Sales Professionals hear it, they immediately associate it with their previous failures and their eyes glaze over.

Inheriting Obstacles

One of the important timesaving aspects of Tactical Prospecting is that it allows you to avoid the wasteful obstacles that lengthen or inhibit the sales process. The opposite is true with typical prospecting methods: the time-wasting obstacles are *inherited* as a by-product of the prospecting behavior itself. Sound strange? Well, let's examine the typical obstacles of a cold call:

Obstacle 1: You need to research and identify a Target customer.

Obstacle 2: You need to bypass a gatekeeper.

Obstacle 3: You need to communicate with a decision-maker.

Obstacle 4: You need to win the trust of the vetting decision-maker.

Obstacle 5: You need to win trust for your company.

Obstacle 6: You need to win trust for your product.

Obstacle 7: You need to overcome incumbent or competitive vendors.

Obstacle 8: You need to overcome price competition.

Obstacle 9: You need to negotiate ancillary issues.

Obstacle 10: You need to negotiate the close.

These are the common steps, disregarding any other potential variables that crop up and delay the sales cycle, such as the decision-maker leaving the company, budget changes, or your own product changes. There are many stumbling points that can and do surface during the process, especially as the sales cycle increases in length. We have always been told that the sales process consists of overcoming objections or obstacles. But where did they come from in the first place? We had no obstacles to overcome prior to identifying a Target customer to prospect. Before beginning the prospecting process for new customers, the Sales Professional had a clean mental path straight to the sales close. So, why is it necessary to create self-imposed burdens purely by instituting a certain prospecting technique, not to mention the burdensome obstacle of a poor-producing prospecting method itself? How could that method possibly make anyone rich or even successful, including the organization?

CHAPTER 2

The Three Principles
of Tactical Prospecting

THE THREE PRINCIPLES OF Tactical Prospecting are the basis required to successfully employ **the Alliance Process**. The first principle is to invest the least amount of time possible when engaging in the prospecting method. The second is to conduct accurate measurements of the methods used. And the third is to identify people with a **Business-Development Mindset**.

> **The Alliance Process:** the process of identifying, engaging, and forming agreed upon business-development relationships with people who will assist in gaining access to Targets.
>
> **A Business-Development Mindset is:**
> 1. The ability to identify an Opportunity.
> 2. The ability to engage an Opportunity.
> 3. The ability to negotiate an Opportunity.

1. The Least Amount of Time

You must assess the necessary tactics required to reduce the amount of time it will take to gain an appointment, especially with methods that are forced on you. That's the most important factor to ascertain: determine how long it's going to take. Next, you must perform *all* the common prospecting methods available to you but engage in the other methods only for an amount of time equal to their success rate. As that is a crucial element with the Alliance Process, it is also a crucial element with other forms of prospecting. If I engage in a form of prospecting that produces one appointment for every fifty attempts, then I shouldn't continue with that activity more than 2 percent of my prospecting time. If it has value, then the success ratio will increase and only at that point should the time allotted also increase. Even if the Alliance Process was initially performed only 2 percent of the time, the ratio of success would increase with the activity. But if you're successful at gaining appointments 2 percent of the time, and that ratio never changes, you shouldn't continue to invest most of your prospecting time in that activity. A prospecting method must earn your time.

It may become apparent that if a prospecting method works only 2 percent of the time, the strategy behind this method must change. If cold calling is designed to be performed over and over to achieve two out of one hundred successes, it would be irrational to think you could make one hundred random attempts only ten minutes out of every eight hours. There would be no point in starting. Obviously, a new perspective on this method would emerge. That perspective would be that it's not worth devising any strategy at all. If a 2 percent success is worthy of only 2 percent of your time, then it should only be performed as an afterthought, a chance byproduct of a more productive activity. Performing an activity only ten minutes a day is basically limited to a "what the heck" approach: *What the heck, I might as well go knock on that door; I'm here anyway.*

2. Realistic Measurement

You must be cognizant of accurate and continual measurement of the methods at every stage of the process engagement. The measurements are honest, accurate data that represent actual results, targeted results, and the measured momentum of activity. It is crucial that the measurements are realistic, not artificially imposed by belief or expected outcomes. The measurement equations will be examined in detail in the upcoming **Alliance Analytics** chapters.

> **Alliance Analytics:** the measurement tools of the Alliance Process.

3. Identify a Business-Development Mindset

There are several characteristics that determine the presence of a **Business-Development Mindset** in people. These characteristics are determined by the individual's behavior and can exist even if the individual is unaware of their own level. It's also possible to point out that there are times when an **Ally** will have little or no awareness that

> **Ally:** a contact with whom you've formed an agreed-upon business development relationship.
> **Access:** having influence over a Target, enabling rapid authoritative interactions

they possess a Mindset at all, and who may simply have **access** to a Target. That's okay as long as you determine that fact early in the relationship and provide the necessary assistance pursuing the Opportunity.

The Business-Development Mindset

The most important characteristic of Tactical Prospecting is identifying people with a Business-Development Mindset or an ability to identify, engage, and negotiate Opportunities. As these characteristics are the bedrock for prospecting, the Business-Development Mindset is a requirement to form Alliances. But specifically, what is a Mindset? Although it's another one of those labels that I can't improve on, I'm not trying to be intentionally ambiguous to escape my responsibility of defining it. A Mindset is defined by its behavior. And like selling, a Mindset to develop business is a talent. It may be a learned talent or, as is often the case, it may be a talent you are born with, but the origin of the talent is meaningless. The importance—and in fact, the success—of this method completely depends on your ability to identify it in others. Basically, what you're looking for is people with the ability to offer Leads that are connected to a Target. Okay, that's what you're looking for, but how do you identify it in others?

I was shopping for supplemental insurance to augment my income in case of unforeseen illness or injury. I met with the insurance agent and she asked a series of questions about my job, the compensation structure, and total income. As a Sales Professional, I explained the need to replace the commission portion of my compensation as that would be the income lost if I couldn't work. She completely understood because her pay structure was a 100 percent commission basis. After reviewing various policies, she recommended a specific insurance plan. She then continued to ask questions about my profession, the type of customers I pursued, the geographic territory, and how I prospected for them.

I could see that she sensed an opportunity that could benefit her prospecting. After I answered her questions, she told me that we both had the same customer types. I suggested a follow-up meeting to review our existing and potential customers to isolate the best prospects and assist each other with gaining appointments.

In the next meeting, she proposed the idea that she could attend my next sales meeting. She then offered to provide one to two of her own customer contacts to each of my twelve sales team members and set up an appointment for them. In exchange, she would present her insurance products to them.

I could tell she had the ability to identify and create a business-development opportunity, so I expanded on her idea. I proposed a plan to prospect for new business. The plan was for the insurance agent and the salesperson to go on the sales appointments together. We would offer our products at a reduced price and apply the credit to any new insurance policies the customers purchased. The customer could buy both products at a reduced price, providing the agent and salesperson an increased chance of closing the sale. The result was that eleven new appointments were gained for the sales team and four new appointments for the insurance agent. This level of production was achieved as a result of a mere two-hour meeting, and a Business-Development Mindset.

The Mindset is defined as an individual possessing the ability to perform these tasks:

1. Identify an Opportunity.

2. Engage an Opportunity.

3. Negotiate an Opportunity.

1. Identify an Opportunity.

When it comes to Tactical Prospecting, an Opportunity is defined as the availability to establish the quickest agreed-upon relationship with a person who has access to your Target. You may identify the Opportunity by yourself, it may pop into your head as an epiphany, or a colleague may point it out to you. I have seen the latter occur in this manner most of the time because a Sales Professional can become overwhelmed with mental obstacles generated by their daily responsibilities. If they simply don't have enough ability to prioritize all the business stimuli encountered as a result, they completely miss the obvious cues.

There was a missed cue when I worked with a colleague who was attempting to cold call his way into a large prospect account. The prospect told him that he must go through their outsourced order fulfillment company that purchases and services those products for them. That's whom he needed to contact. I realized that the outsourced company was a perfect POS Partner Ally, as it had hundreds of other similar accounts as their client base. But the Sales Professional didn't make the connection. He was too focused on making the sale to the single prospect company. After several failed attempts to set up a Webinar appointment with the outsourced order fulfillment company, he asked me for assistance. I took a quick look at the outsourced company and realized right away that they possessed a massive database of clients that he could access through an Alliance relationship. I told my colleague not to limit his thinking to the single prospect account. The potential to engage hundreds of other prospect accounts was enormous if he could establish an agreed-upon relationship with the outsourced company.

As diagrammed below, you can see with the same effort and much less time, he could gain access to a larger multiple of prospects with a greater closing ratio simply by identifying the Opportunity for the immense potential that it had.

The Typical Prospecting Path

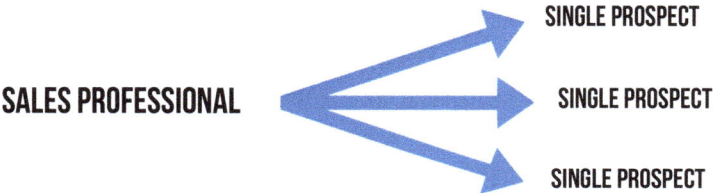

SALES PROFESSIONAL

SINGLE PROSPECT

SINGLE PROSPECT

SINGLE PROSPECT

The Tactical Prospecting Path

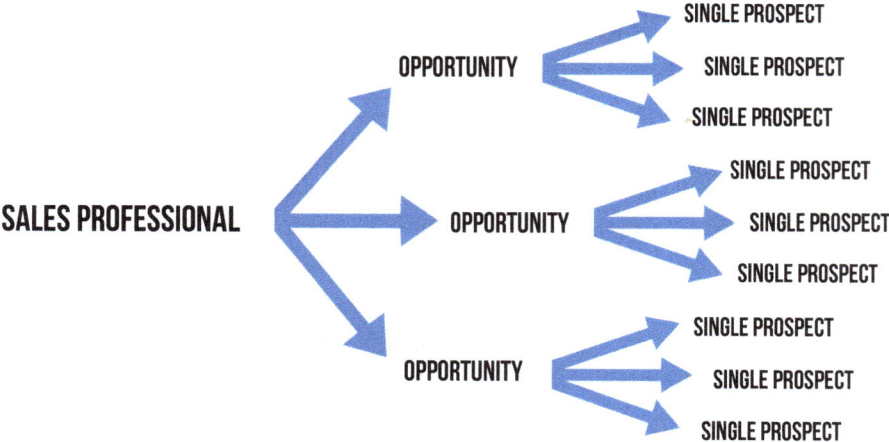

SALES PROFESSIONAL

OPPORTUNITY

SINGLE PROSPECT

SINGLE PROSPECT

SINGLE PROSPECT

OPPORTUNITY

SINGLE PROSPECT

SINGLE PROSPECT

SINGLE PROSPECT

OPPORTUNITY

SINGLE PROSPECT

SINGLE PROSPECT

SINGLE PROSPECT

2. Engage the Opportunity.

Properly engaging an Opportunity means employing the most facilitative communication method in the fastest manner possible. The speed of engagement is completely based on an understanding of the Opportunity's power. If the productivity potential of an Opportunity is understood, then the desire to form the Alliance relationship should be powerful enough to exchange information with no delay and prevent anything from standing in your way.

Continuing with the story, by the time I finished describing the productivity potential of the Ally, I saw a lightbulb over his head. Unfortunately, it was a real lightbulb hanging over our table. In other words, he still didn't get it. I finally demanded, "Stop setting up Webinar meetings, go there, meet with them; it's worth the two-hour drive." Subsequently, a meeting was established, and I assisted with the presentation remotely by phone. The result was that the Management company identified and provided a list of seventy-nine out of their three hundred clients as a Target match for the product; eighty if you count the original prospect.

Virtually, every one of the seventy-nine clients would become appointments because their trusted consultant outsourced company told them to meet with us. And because of the extremely high closing rate of these Ally appointments, the calculated average would become fifty sales. Now the question is, knowing and believing these metrics ahead of time, would any Sales Professional make multiple attempts to send invites for a Webinar, or would he immediately try to meet them face to face—even if they had to hitchhike there? Also, as you can see, when an Ally isolates Target prospects and provides them to you, the concept of a near, net-zero amount of prospecting time becomes apparent. Calculate the amount of prospecting time it took to reach the original single Target account and divide it by eighty.

3. Negotiate the Opportunity.

The ability to negotiate an Opportunity is based on understanding the factors important to that Target as well as understanding the resources you have available to offer. It is the ultimate compromise between what they need and what you need, as determined by what they can give and what you can give. But it is also based on an ability to gather information about the Target to determine what is and isn't important to them. Simply put, the successful negotiation is striking an equal balance while convincing the other party that they received a greater benefit.

One time, I was negotiating a new contract with a real estate management company for communications equipment. Ten years earlier, they had purchased the equipment and paid a monthly maintenance fee, as was standard in the industry at the time. As the industry rates changed over the years, the pricing structure completely flipped to the point where it was less expensive to lease the equipment and pay for the service than they were paying just in monthly-service fees alone without having to purchase the product. Upon realizing the years of overpayment, the president of the company was angry and wanted my head. So, I worked out a special deal that satisfied the "wants" of both parties.

I converted their contract to a lease and lowered the rate to the prevailing lease rate. Then I reduced it a few dollars more and used that difference as a credit to buy back the equipment. After eighteen months, the total credits would be equal to the value of the purchased equipment and my company would re-own it from them. At that point, the monthly rate would be raised to the standard lease rate. We were crediting a few dollars a month per unit to the customer, in the form of a reduced rate, to purchase my equipment back from them.

Instead of a lease/purchase, I flipped the arrangement and probably created the world's first purchase/lease agreement. The true balance struck was that they received a below-market monthly rate for the product, which represented our payment to them to buy back the equipment. The perceived imbalance in favor of the customer was receiving a below-market rate for the product to compensate for the earlier overpayment.

They believed they got their money back. They saved $12,000 per year in service payments simply by agreeing to transfer ownership of the equipment back to us. That was the equipment they had no advantage to own or need to own.

The Comparison of the Balance Achieved with the Purchase/Lease Deal:

Customer Wants	Vendor Wants
- Keep the same equipment.	- Save the account.
- Lower the rates.	- Maintain rates that were profitable.
- Achieve mental satisfaction for years of overpayment.	- Provide a balance that satisfies both parties.

This mental balance is often encountered when a customer believes they have been overcompensated and got the better end of the deal.

The reason some people possess the Mindset, and some don't, may be an interesting topic to discuss, but it is irrelevant when it comes to Tactical Prospecting. The only thing that matters is the ability to identify the existence and the level of this talent in others.

Identifying the Mindset

How do we recognize the ability to identify, engage, and negotiate opportunities? Well, we can't read people's minds, but we can read their behavior. And their behavior provides the metrics used to identify the proper Mindset of an Ally, before your intuition is strong enough to do that on its own. Those metrics are volume and frequency of quality Leads they provide. And I mean "quality" in the sales life-and-death sense, not in the alliterative sense, simply because the term flows nicely after you say the word "quantity." I'll provide a better description of a "qualified" prospect below.

A qualified prospect originating from an Ally has three elements:

1. A need for the product.

2. A willingness to purchase the product.

3. An ability to purchase the product.

And to be a qualified prospect for a sale, they must possess *all* three things.

I came across this when I was working on a large deal with a family-owned electrical contractor. The company name took on the family name—for example, "Smith and Family Electrical." From the start of the sales process, I was dealing with the son, whom we'll call Joe Smith. He ran the day-to-day operations and was one of the key decision-makers. I say "one of the key decision-makers" because, as you will see, he thought of himself as the sole decision-maker. Unfortunately, I did as well, mainly because there was a large sign in the lobby right over the receptionist's head that read:

"Joe Smith is the Boss and the Decisions Stop with Joe Smith."

It should have said, "The Buck Stops with Joe Smith." But as you'll see, the sign didn't because the buck didn't. After three months of back-and-forth negotiating, he called me and said, "Okay, let's do the deal." I prepared all the equipment and brought it to the location along with the contract to be signed.

When I got there, I waited for over an hour in the lobby while the receptionist buzzed his phone, reminding him that I was still waiting. Finally, the receptionist was buzzed back; she hung up and said, "Mr. Smith won't be coming out." She added in a scripted tone, "He's no longer interested." I kept calm at first and asked to just speak with him simply to get an explanation. She said he wouldn't come out.

Now I was furious. I said, "I gotta speak to him—he just wasted three months of my time."

The receptionist then leaned over her counter and whispered to me, "He's not really in charge, his mother makes all the decisions. She canceled the order."

As the consummate Sales Professional, I swallowed my pride and thought of ways to save the deal. My first hope was that it was one of those Norman Bates scenarios, the character from a horror film, where he and his mother were the same person . . . maybe I could get him to sign once he took off the dress.

I waited a bit longer, then I regained my senses and admitted to myself that the deal was truly lost. I stood up and defiantly asked the receptionist for a piece of tape. I took out the contract, tore it in half, and taped it onto the sign. I covered the end of the sentence, and all that was left showing were the words . . .

"Joe Smith is the Boss and the Decisions Stop—"

Now, Joe Smith might have had a need for the product, and was willing to buy the product, but he certainly had no ability to. And when it comes to a qualified prospect, two out of three is bad.

How to Determine Mindset Strength

The strength of a person's Mindset can be determined only by their behavior. A simple question and answer can be used for an initial assessment, while their future productivity will determine the strength and the category over the long term. The characteristic strengths:

Strongest Mindset is in those that offer Leads without you asking.

Mid-level Mindset is in those that offer Leads after asking.

Weakest Mindset is in those who don't offer Leads with or without asking. And just like a tough sales call, this is the situation in which more selling techniques are employed to gain access to their Contacts.

A Mindset isn't limited to any single profession or industry or to any other stereotyped identification. I can provide a multitude of examples—many of which are my existing Allies—of professionals in non-sales positions who are fantastic at identifying, engaging, and negotiating the Opportunities. And, ironically, the opposite is also true. There are plenty of Sales Professionals who remain in the profession and literally can't identify an Opportunity even after it's found, engaged, and negotiated for them. I've seen situations when these Opportunities are handed right to them, and the Sales Professional didn't believe it was worth keeping the appointment.

And even more common are the Sales Professionals who defend to the death all the other typical prospecting methods but derive the bulk of their sales from some form of Tactical Prospecting and don't even know it. I can provide a multitude of examples that are too numerous to list. But some will be discussed later in the book. But regarding the three principles of Tactical Prospecting, this belief manifests itself predominantly in the third principle: identifying an Ally with a Business-Development Mindset.

Take Tactical Control

Now by itself, determining the expended time and resulting success rate of a method that you're utilizing voluntarily isn't always the ultimate prospecting solution. The problem surfaces when you are saddled with mandatory, low-producing methods that require a ton of time. And the amount of time used is not merely the raw number of hours taken up by an exceptionally low attempts-to-success ratio. The time loss is compounded by the slowed **momentum** after multiple failing attempts. The drop-off in momentum is due to loss of concentration and motivation, and all the side effects experienced when engaging in perceived futility. This momentum is more than a feeling; as you will see, it is a deficit-producing quantifiable value. Being saddled with tasks ripe with limitations can come in many forms but can be resolved with simple tactics.

> **Momentum:** the quantity of potential revenue movement that translates into the loss or gain of prospecting time.

Prospecting Limitations

Data Limitation

A Sales Professional can be limited by resources in the form of inaccurate data, obsolete data, or no data at all. In each case, the Sales Professional will have to develop their own data, and unfortunately, the research time adds to the expended prospecting task time. The limitation of any resource is only relative to what the competition has. I point this out because the tools and their effectiveness must be accurately determined, otherwise, the Sales Professional becomes the guinea pig for the expected work ethic that Management projects onto them. If the competition is prospecting in the same manner with the same historical success rate, then having better data will increase their ratio over yours, even slightly. If they can gain one additional appointment from one hundred attempts, that becomes a one out of fifty and cuts their time in half.

The **Resolution Tactic** is to do your own research:

Develop your own data from existing account types, industry verticals, and potential new Targets from an untapped market segment. If you can identify new, untapped customers for your product, it will provide a tremendous time advantage because it knocks out the incumbent obstacle and the competition obstacle. Also, it provides the prospect an additional advantage over their competition that they hadn't thought of.

The Mandatory Method Limitation

The required prospecting method itself is a limitation if it historically produces a low success rate. The most common example of this is cold-calling efforts that come in all forms and carry with them an expectation of a large time investment. If you know that one hundred attempts of some behavior will take eight hours and will gain one success, then even if you change the technique and the rate of success remains the same, the eight-hour time investment per success will also stay the same. If you can't change the success rate, you must change the amount of time it takes to attain that success. And to do that, you must change the method used to deliver the one hundred attempts. A simple example is if I made one hundred telemarketing calls and left eighty-two voicemails, there is certainly a faster way to deliver eighty-two messages to prospects than by calling each one. And by avoiding all the inane voicemail messaging gimmicks, such as the "Short and Sweet," "The Name Last," or any other ridiculous "I fooled you into calling me back" techniques, this method will compensate with the immense time savings.

The **Resolution Tactic** is to use outside agents to perform initial cold-calling activity:

This can be in the form of professional telemarketers, marketing tools, and at the most basic, email marketing. When these and other techniques are employed, then the wasted hours are transferred to a different entity and the resulting successes are transferred to you. The appointment success ratio from an outside agent is astronomically higher because those transferred have already agreed to a meeting at some level, and your time invested is astronomically lower.

Designated Resources Limitation

The limitation by designated resources takes the form of databases that have no match to the proper Target. If you're required to work entire lists of prospects that have little chance of matching the need for your product, your supervisor may say there's a jewel that was missed. In other words, somewhere in the list there is a match. Even if that's true, with the bulk of prospects having little chance of producing an appointment, searching for their jewel will take up too much of *your* jewel: your time.

The **Resolution Tactic** is to immediately determine if these resources are constructive or destructive:

Prospect to a random sample of 10 percent of the data, either by randomly choosing them or by simply alphabetizing the list and attacking the first 10 percent in order. Of course, be efficient with your analysis; if the list is prohibitively long, then the random sample can be reduced, and if it's too short, then it can be increased, even to the point of prospecting the entire database, if short enough. Even with a very small database, the general feedback will give an idea if the database is the correct Target. The percentage of results will accurately extrapolate across the entire database, and you'll discover what you're dealing with. Also, a positive result is anything at all that contributes to a positive movement toward the goal. It can be new information, new people, or anything gained that warrants further investigation to definitively ascertain the Target's value.

Isolated Market Limitation

If you're required to work a specific vertical or territory, this can be limiting for several reasons. Its buying habits may have changed, the base may be saturated, or your competition may be attacking the market with the same tactics. Then every breathing Sales Professional in the market is repeatedly messaging every breathing decision-maker. Also, what will be shown with the Alliance Process is the negative impact presented by the boundary restrictions. Because when tactically prospecting, potential Allies and their potential Opportunities are not limited to a territory.

The **Resolution Tactic** is to surreptitiously prospect outside the vertical or territory:

The resulting success may be accepted by supervisors and rewarded in the form of expansion into the new areas or, if necessary, splitting deals with the local Sales Professional. If you split enough deals, there's a chance you'll inherit those new areas as well once your supervisor realizes where the existing Sales Professional has been getting the

> **Lead:** a person who has access to a Target.

new business. Unfortunately, those are big "ifs and maybes" because it's also possible that the structure of the organization's sales process is too stifling, in which case *your* supervisor won't try to realize anything and will simply cheat you.

The Best Resolution Tactic: Limit the Limitation

Avoid the low-success-rate prospecting methods as much as possible in the first place, or at least until the high-success/low-time Tactical Prospecting methods can be perfected and pick up the slack.

Remain Principled

The original impetus for developing Tactical Prospecting and the Alliance Process was the need to produce faster in a restrictive sales environment. All types of obstacles will always be present in one form or another as old ones get replaced with the new. The only variation will be the level of restriction and the level to which productivity is affected. Regardless of whether the restrictions are omnipresent or change, the principles of Tactical Prospecting are standards to remain independent of the pitfalls and to completely avoid the restrictions. By adopting a Tactical Prospecting mentality, you will have no need for the simple resolutions because the smart ones will be waiting.

PART TWO

Real Hunting

Instituting the Alliance Process

THE GENERIC TERM "hunter" describes Sales Professionals who focus solely on identifying and acquiring new business. The Alliance Process is the new way of engaging in this prospecting practice. The foundation principle is hunting for the people who will assist in gaining access to Targets that provide a level of prospecting productivity. This process consists of instituting methods and tactics to find the people with the strongest Business-Development Mindset and forming an agreed-upon relationship with them. So, the first step in this prospecting process is to research and identify those human beings who can help gain access to a Target. The Target can be any form of prospecting productivity including, and ideally, an existing customer. For these people, the characteristics of their Mindset must be identified, measured, and either assigned to a specific Ally category or set aside. The function of the Alliance Process is to create a permanent, interactive base of people with whom you have an agreed-upon relationship for business development, and the resulting output will be a perpetual flow of Leads of superior quality.

Since existing Allies in your personal database will already possess the Business-Development Mindset—otherwise they would not be Allies—newly prospected people must fulfill the Mindset requirements necessary to be categorized as an Ally. The result of forming the relationship is always a positive gain in productivity because an Ally doesn't interact with you unless they have something to offer.

To achieve success with the Alliance Process, it is crucial that the Sales Professional first believe this prospecting technique is a viable alternative to common methods. However, the resulting metrics will ultimately prove that they must begin *without* a preconceived association with the other common methods labeled "networking."

Once Allies are formed, a myriad of resulting business growth mechanisms can be used to reach other key Targets that are associated with them in some way. A Target can be any entity that provides some form of productivity, including new information, new Opportunities, or other human beings with access to other Targets. The various mechanisms that can be employed in the Alliance Process are limited only by the creative desire of the hunter and the resources proportional to the value of the end goal.

CHAPTER 3

Building the Prospecting Machine

Eliminating Obstacles

THE FIRST ADVANTAGE to this form of prospecting is the elimination of unnecessary cursory steps that expend time. Whereas typical prospecting activities create obstacles merely by the nature of their methods, when employing the Alliance Process, you are receiving qualified Opportunities from people with strong Business-Development Mindsets with most, if not all, of the inherited prospecting obstacles eliminated. Let's revisit the cold-call obstacles with a Lead that is generated through the Alliance Process:

Obstacle 1: You need to research and identify a Target customer.

Obstacle 2: You need to bypass a gatekeeper.

Obstacle 3: You need to communicate with a decision-maker.

Obstacle 4: You need to win the trust of the vetting decision-maker.

Obstacle 5: You need to win the trust for your company.

Obstacle 6: You need to win the trust for your product.

Obstacle 7: You need to overcome incumbent or competitive vendors.

Obstacle 8: You need to overcome price competition.

Obstacle 9: You need to negotiate ancillary issues.

Obstacle 10: You need to negotiate the close.

Eliminated Obstacle 1: Research and identify a Target customer.

There is no Target identification process necessary because the Ally provides the Lead and, in some cases, becomes the Target themselves.

Eliminated Obstacle 2: Need to bypass a gatekeeper.

There is no gatekeeper to bypass and no vetting for the decision-makers because the Ally is the vetting entity and establishes the introduction themselves.

Eliminated Obstacle 3: Need to communicate with a decision-maker.

There is no need for repetitive touches to communicate because the Target decision-maker is expecting the communication.

Eliminated Obstacle 4: Need to win the trust of the vetting decision-maker.

There is no need for any product introduction because the prospect already has the need. Otherwise, the identification of the need never would have been made by the Ally. Of course, product descriptions and demonstrations will be necessary.

Eliminated Obstacle 5: Need to win the trust for your company.

There isn't a need to win trust because you have been recommended by an individual Ally who is already trusted by the prospect. **However, you must do what is expected, otherwise, you can easily lose the trust!**

Eliminated Obstacle 6: You need to win the trust for your product.

There isn't a need to earn product trust for the same reason as number five; however, the product must be shown to meet their needs. The Alliance Process gets you the appointment and greatly increases the closing percentage, if by nothing else, virtually eliminating a sales cycle.

Eliminated Obstacle 7: Need to overcome incumbent or competitive vendors.

The obstacle posed by incumbent vendors or the competition is eliminated as well. The comfort level and familiarity of an incumbent vendor is matched by their comfort level with the Ally. And the competition is eliminated because there is little to no familiarity with an outside vendor, and as a result, the same comfort level doesn't exist. Also, and more importantly, the competition may be burdened with the same obstacles that their own prospecting methods have created.

Eliminated Obstacle 8: Need to overcome price competition.

The price issue is reduced with negotiation or is eliminated because the comfort and trust will translate into the necessary value.

Eliminated Obstacle 9: Need to negotiate ancillary issues.

The ancillary obstacles will never appear because these obstacles are a byproduct of the prospecting method. They are also a byproduct of a sales cycle that, as mentioned, is virtually eliminated. By "virtually eliminated," I mean reduced to a level of insignificance. There is always some time associated with the sales process, but if the time is reduced by 90 percent, would a sales cycle even be a consideration of any of the procedures associated with the process? For instance, if the sales cycle goes from twenty-four weeks to two weeks, wouldn't forecasting, quota, and inventory Management all become a nearly insignificant consideration?

Eliminated Obstacle 10: Need to negotiate the close.

The only obstacle that is posed with Tactical Prospecting is the negotiation. With the Alliance Process, 90 percent of the sale is closed before you walk in the door; the last 10 percent is negotiation. Now, of course it is possible that the potential customer doesn't buy even if they have the need. And the reasons are exhaustive and really nothing that could have been anticipated.

But this is the key point with prospecting customers in this manner: even if the purchasing obstacle could be discovered prior to the appointment and it was guaranteed that the prospect for whatever reason wasn't going to purchase, that is still a good appointment. Why? With Tactical Prospecting, there is never an unproductive sales call. The Contact established can become a new Ally. And with this new Ally, you can **Anchor Seed** by offering Leads to them, or give them access to their Targets in exchange for the same from them in the future. Also, the original prospect will eventually purchase when their own buying obstacles no longer exist. With the strong Ally relationship you've formed, when they're ready to buy, whom do you think they'll call first?

> **Anchor Seed:** offering Leads to an Ally before receiving Leads.

Common Prospecting Complaints

There are many reasons why typical prospecting methods are fraught with limitations in their methodology and, unfortunately, go unchallenged. Over time, I have heard a myriad of justifications for the poor appointment-producing results. I have listed some of the most frequent complaints, which you can keep in the back of your mind for now. As I said earlier, if I do my job, then at the end of this reading, you will be able to review these complaints again and realize they have no place in the world of Allies.

So, why haven't you made any appointments?

Complaint 1: I can't get by the receptionist.

Complaint 2: Our price is too high.

Complaint 3: Nobody knows us.

Complaint 4: The economy is slow.

Complaint 5: I don't have my business cards yet.

The last complaint is one I've heard the most as the excuse for delaying any prospecting activity. I've also heard "the business cards are laminated, so I can't write any notes on them."

As a side note, some advice for the die-hard cold callers: if you refuse to give up cold calling and want to get better at it, my only suggestion would be to try it without business cards. You'll then concentrate more on the interaction taking place, listen better, and respond accordingly. When the prospect asks for your business card, it means you haven't communicated anything of interest, and it's their way of closing the door on you.

The Real Deal

As promised, to fulfill my obligation to you, I will provide the steps for building a prospecting machine consisting of long-term Allies that provide Leads or access to your Targets on a continuous basis. That is the key: once formed, Allies produce a volume of Leads that will reduce the net time that was invested to create the original Ally to virtually zero. Think about that concept for a moment. Imagine prospecting for appointments that required truly little time or no time at all. You may ask, how can you generate an appointment that didn't use any time? Simple. Someone else generated it for you. And that's what the Alliance Process will do.

One day I had a sales colleague come into my office at the end of the day. Feeling proud of himself, he raised his arms and triumphantly proclaimed that he had made seventy-four telephone cold calls that day and got two appointments. And I replied, "I got two appointments today, and I didn't make any cold calls." Which was the case.

The Components of the Alliance Process

The components of the Alliance Process are the parts of a structured prospecting mechanism. They are consistent in their definition, allowing for consistency in their results. This creates a formal process for interaction and measurement. On the surface, the components may appear to be abstract, but when they are defined in both identification and behavior, they become concrete elements of a process. The working parts form a mechanism designed to identify people with a talent to develop business, to take the actions to engage these individuals, and to produce the permanent result of forming an ongoing business-development relationship with them. That agreed-upon relationship will become the perpetual source of Leads. The Components of the Process:

A Significant Interaction

A **communication** with the purposes of **business development** in the form of identifying, engaging, or negotiating Opportunities.

A Target

Any entity with which you can **gain any level of prospecting productivity** or movement toward the goal. A Target can include a prospect organization, an individual person, or a piece of information.

A Lead

A **person** who has **access to a Target** with which you have had no previous **significant interaction**.

A Contact

A **Lead** after you have **had any type of significant interaction**.

An Ally

A **Contact** with whom you have **an agreed-upon relationship** for **business development**.

The agreed-upon relationship can be business or social in

nature and can include anyone from acquaintances to friends to business associates. The agreed-upon relationship is a vehicle for exchanging Leads on a perpetual basis. This relationship can remain productive and long-lasting even if the Ally is never aware of their status as an Ally component.

In practice, the components define the individuals and guide the necessary actions according to their place in the process. For instance, here is an example of the process steps used in a previous hunting position:

Component 1: A Lead

A professional sports team marketing executive emailed my company's marketing department attempting to sell us advertising. Our marketing manager responded with a snotty attitude, basically stating that we don't advertise to the typical sports consumer, and even if we did, it wouldn't be with your team. Since the team was situated in my region, the email was forwarded to me as a responsibility-delegation brush-off, with the undeniable expectation by our marketing manager that it would go nowhere. However, I saw an Opportunity. Due to the rude nature of the communication and the marketing executive's—the Lead's—desire to form a business-development relationship, I believed that I had enough political capital to start out with the advantage to fuel the Opportunity so . . .

Component 2: A Significant Interaction

I called the team's marketing executive, and we discussed possible ways to satisfy his requirements—the Significant Interaction. But what was more important to me was to uncover his level of Business-Development Mindset. I guessed that the team's owner had become wealthy through some type of separate business enterprise, which could be a potential customer. This turned out to be the case. Through our discussions, I learned that the team owner also built and owned an international manufacturing company that was a perfect Target match for the service I was selling . . .

Component 3: A Target

As Opportunity (typically called "luck") would have it, the timing of our meeting was the residue of the process. Their front office Management communicated a directive to their marketing personnel. The company, the professional sports team, and all the associated parties were told to use the manufacturing company as a bargaining tool to help sell advertising for the sports team. The owner's company would be willing to purchase vendors' products as goodwill, in exchange for the vendors purchasing team advertising. Although we had no use for advertising to their Target consumer at that point, a creative Opportunity surfaced. The marketing executive set up a meeting with the CIO of the manufacturing company—the Target.

Component 4: A Contact

I developed a tactical plan for the marketing executive—now the Contact—that would satisfy my company, the manufacturing company, and the sports team. If I could sell the CIO of the manufacturing company our service, I would pay the sports team a residual commission as a reseller of our service, and those funds would be escrowed, to be used as advertising dollars at a later time when our company was ready to advertise to sports consumers. Since the marketing executive possessed a Business-Development Mindset, which was the only reason this succeeded, he understood perfectly and got the plan approved by his VP of marketing . . .

Component 5: An Ally

We continued building the plan to include the other manufacturers in the vertical, who were their customers. I was given access to these other manufacturers by the marketing executive (who at this point has become the Ally) to also sell them my service, which in turn would generate more advertising dollars in the form of residual payments to the professional sports team. Everyone wins.

This scenario may appear to be creatively convoluted; however, that strengthens my point. Could such an unconventional solution to a business problem between two parties with misaligned objectives have any chance of succeeding unless the components of the Alliance Process were employed?

The 3 Principles of the Alliance Process

1. Hunt for People
2. Categorize
3. Use Selling Techniques

1. Hunt for People

I'd like to make what's obvious, obvious. Everyone probably knows it but won't admit it. People are the key — not arbitrary directories, industry lists, random office visits, or any other inanimate sales tools. The best directory that ever existed is a person's brain. And your job is to get access to the Contacts in that brain. With a Tactical Mentality, the first step in the prospecting process should be to pursue Target people, not organizations. Typically, the first step when prospecting for customers is to either identify businesses you'd like to sell to or just randomly pursue non-specific businesses through trial-and-error communicating. But when such randomization methods are initiated, the Sales Professional has officially entered the prospecting obstacle course and immediately falls victim to the resulting metrics.

This is not to say that an organization isn't ever an initial Target. Sometimes there are known advantages with a specific organization that permits bypassing any obstructions. However, this isn't the case most of the time, unless you make it so. It's just more productive to pursue people in industries that match your Target customers than it is to pursue a single, specific organization first. By hunting specific organizations, the Sales Professional limits the number of potential Leads that can be generated in a specified time. For instance, if an IT professional is a good Target decision-maker for an IT product you're selling, there are many of these professionals within a specified industry. And a single Target IT professional can provide access to multiple other IT professionals who can be engaged and communicated with and who can provide access to sell to a multitude of organizations.

As you will learn, the objective of communicating with a key individual Lead isn't to sell them; it's to identify their Mindset and create an Ally. Once that's done, the new Ally can offer other people as Opportunities. Also, by initially targeting multiple people of the same type—by profession, industry, or any parameter you determine to be significantly relevant—their own organizations also become potential end-user customer Opportunities. You create not only a direct, unencumbered route to their Contacts but also a direct prospecting route into their company. But equally important, in each case, the typical prospecting obstacles are bypassed and avoided. In contrast, if an organization is pursued first, then all the typical obstacles are encountered and must be overcome. The cascade of inefficiency continues with the next organization and the next. Ultimately, you're spending your time figuring out how to overcome obstacles when you should have already avoided them in the first place. Remember, to have the best return on investment of time—our most important asset—our prospecting needs to be efficient.

Since the targeted person's organization also becomes a potential customer for the product, you are creating a Lead-generating Ally and an end-user customer in a single pass. If it turns out that they're a match for your product and you penetrate the account with the original intention of forming an Ally, then is there any concern about bypassing the gatekeeper or overcoming any of the other problems encountered with common prospecting methods? Some of these I mentioned earlier: the gatekeeper, the competition, no business cards. All are obstacles created by trying to introduce yourself to strangers who may or may not be ready to purchase your product. And if the new person, who was referred by an Ally, isn't ready to purchase, they can become an Ally and tell you about others. In contrast, if I prospect the old way and need to research organizations, communicate with organizations, report on organizations, follow up on organizations, and hopefully gain appointments with organizations, then I'm completely dependent on picking the correct organizations. Otherwise, my time is invested researching, contacting, reporting, following up, and visiting, with a single-digit percentage return on my investment.

Of course, the value of the person as a Lead-generating entity is still dependent on their Mindset. So, after creating a **Significant Interaction** with the proper Contacts and forming the Ally relationship, the reservoir of Leads in their biological database will seem omnipotent, due to either their volume or speed to success. They will know the "who," either quickly—due to the Target's immediate need—or in abundance—due to the vast number of Targets that are offered.

There is a counterintuitive and somewhat unique selling perspective associated with the Alliance Process. By targeting a person first rather than an organization, the customers are brought to you with little or no prior identification of them. Instead of deciding which organizations you would like to sell to, they are decided for you. Ultimately, you realize that it really doesn't matter who buys from you, and you don't need to know what the organizations will be at the beginning of the prospecting process. If your product is designed for a specific industry, why does it matter which specific organizations from that industry become a prospect, then an appointment, then a sale? Let's revisit an earlier story with that concept in mind.

It's like when a VP of sales was reciting a tale that I can almost guarantee he didn't experience firsthand. A salesperson drove by ABC Company every morning and proclaimed that, one day, he was going to sell them his product and nothing was going to stand in his way. The salesperson called, and knocked, and emailed, and "flyered," and tried all the typical methods to communicate. Then finally, after four years, he broke through, got an appointment, and ultimately made the sale. Success! We were all supposed to be inspired to do the same. That may sound like an inspiring story, but for one thing, I can assure you that during the four-year process, he either had other sales or a rich spouse to sustain him while waiting for that specific one. And I can also assure you that those other self-sustaining sales were not prospected in the same manner.

But that's all okay, so long as you devote only the same percentage of time equal to the method's success rate. If 1 percent of your prospecting time is devoted to the "whale," and after four years of selling other customers you succeed in selling the "whale," that's also okay. What isn't okay is trying to portray singular perseverance as the sole technique for chasing all prospects. There is no way that VP would do the same thing in the same situation. Never! But he'd spend four years training you to. How many hundreds of other salespeople drove by that same company, proclaiming the same thing, and didn't accomplish anything other than a PIP or termination letter from their supervisor? No sales story ever ends without supporting the storyteller's method.

Instead, what if other companies just like that one were brought to you without your prior ambition of closing that specific one? Would it matter to you? Would it matter if a company with the same size and revenue and buying capacity agreed to an appointment without your prior prediction of conquest? You can always aspire to closing a large company, but would you care which one it is?

So, how do you find the right Targets that provide, thousands of times, the return on investment of the other methods? You need to build an Alliance base of people that will provide the customers who can be easily accessed, are ready to buy, and are comfortably familiar with you. The rest is just negotiation.

2. Categorize

Once the Business-Development Mindset is initially identified in others as a general aptitude to manage Opportunities, the level of Mindset becomes the second key element in establishing the Ally. To obtain the greatest production from an Ally, their Mindset characteristics must be ascertained as quickly and as accurately as possible. The Ally is then placed in an Ally category that matches this level. Just like selling techniques, where the sales method is dependent on the characteristics and situation with the prospect, the interactions that take place must be associated with the category characteristics. These attributes provide a guide when engaging an Ally for Leads.

As the components of Allies can be viewed as cogs in a gear, the categories should be viewed as the gears of the prospecting machine. Placing the Ally in the correct category is one of the most crucial elements of the Alliance Process. Done incorrectly, it can create many wasted interactions. There are very specific category types and subsequently very specific ways of interacting with them. To create the most useful interactions, you first must understand the five categories:

Ally Categories

1. Passive Ally

2. Process Ally

3. Partner Ally

4. Party Ally

5. Point-of-Sale Ally

3. Use Selling Techniques

The techniques for gaining Allies are the same as the techniques for making sales. For instance, researching, probing, negotiating, and closing are among some of the selling steps that are directed toward the potential Ally. The categories will provide a guide when interacting with an Ally, such as using subtlety, creativity, or directness. Just as one would engage varying techniques with the different customers you are selling to, a large potential deal would be handled differently than a small deal and differently than an existing customer. The Mindset level of the Ally as determined by their category provides an indication of which selling techniques are best used to access their Leads.

How to Employ Selling Techniques with Tactical Prospecting

I have no intention of discussing any selling techniques, nor do I believe that the topic should even be discussed in a sales training venue until prospecting methods are taught. However, in this case, I need to offer two post-prospecting selling methods that are employed in the beginning of the prospecting process, because they directly affect Tactical Prospecting and are a necessary part of it.

The Invisible Shield

The Invisible Shield is a term I created that has an ironic twist in its name. In my experience, I've encountered this behavior from the thousands of potential customers I've called on as a type of defense during a business engagement. The reticence of a customer to reveal facts during an interaction is the Invisible Shield. It's a mental protection that prevents certain sales communications from entering the prospect's comfort zone, as if they want to defend against being "sold." A secondary effect of the shield is that it also prevents the prospect from allowing information to escape. The result is the prospect may not hear pertinent information offered in the sales discussion and, even more importantly, it prevents the Sales Professional from gaining important information in return. Why is it ironic? Well, even though it's an intangible thing, just an attitude, I swear when it is in action, I can almost *see* it. So, how is the Invisible Shield overcome? With Misdirection.

Misdirection

Utilizing and perfecting the technique of Misdirection is extremely helpful with the Tactical Prospecting process, as it helps the Sales Professional gain access to the database of information locked up in an Ally's brain. Misdirection is diverting the discussion with a prospect from the original intent to have them inadvertently provide the necessary information. It will appear as if the prospect came up with answers themselves rather than being led to that place in the dialogue.

The technique is to break the conversation in some manner, either by appearing to end it or altering the topic to create a different route to the goal. For instance, if I secretly knew ahead of time that a customer wanted to break into a new market or sell their products to a new customer, I could superficially mention those items as an anecdote, knowing its importance to them. This would allow the Invisible Shield to drop. Then I could redirect the conversation via these topics toward something important to them. Once the shield drops, I bring it back toward my goal. Ending a conversation, then abruptly restarting another with a nonrelated topic, accomplishes the same thing. There's no desire to end the conversation, it's just used as Misdirection toward your intended topic.

Now, if proper research was done in advance of the meeting, you'd know where to direct the prospect to offer the needed information that won't be protected by the shield. This technique works because first, by waiting until the end of the meeting, the person has already begun to relax and "let down their guard," misdirected into believing that the meeting is over. One way to implement the power of this technique is to rhetorically ask for permission for one more piece of information. By asking permission for "one more thing," this completely disarms the individual because it evokes a helpless sympathy for the Sales Professional, which is difficult for most people to avoid. It also stirs curiosity in them, wondering what the question may be. Also, there's a kind of competitive negotiating greed, believing they can also gain unsolicited information from the Sales Professional. If I have uttered this phrase once, I have uttered it ten thousand times at the end of a meeting, "Let me ask you this . . ." They always let me ask, and they always respond with honest and valuable information. They can't resist allowing the question and then, by an almost uncontrollable reflex, their answer is honest and unencumbered. You can almost hear the Invisible Shield hit the floor.

Allies Quota

I am using the term *quota* for its familiarity only, not for its believed value in the sales process. As it relates to Tactical Prospecting, it is very important to have a goal set within some period to achieve a preset number of Allies. This is true especially for the Sales Professional with few existing customers due to lack of tenure or territory. Of course, the sale is the goal, but during the selling process, there will be a disproportionate ratio of prospects to sales while building the customer base. The way to convert prospects to closed sales is to first develop the base of Allies. So, initially, in addition to a sales goal there should also exist an Allies goal and the two should balance. For example, if the total sales goal is fifty, the Sales Professional should have a combination of Allies and sales that equal fifty. Now a disproportionate level will skew toward the Allies initially until you start turning the Leads they provide into sales and then the balance will shift—40 Allies: 10 sales; 25 Allies: 25 sales; 10 Allies: 40 sales—until the balance shifts.

A word of warning at this point—when the sales-to-Allies ratio shifts in the opposite direction, you'll now be spending a disproportionate amount of time closing sales and have less time to hunt for more Allies. I'm not stating this as a phony sales motivator. The Ally quota needs to be maintained to keep growing. Please don't think of it as keeping a single "funnel full." Think of it as building an Ally base of many individual funnels if we're forced to use that term. Remember that with Allies, the funnels are upside down, so for each category, the Ally is at the top and a great multitude of Leads at the bottom.

Okay, that's it. That is the only post-prospecting sales training I'll offer. In fact, as they're extremely important tools used in the process of building Allies, they're really part of both the prospecting process and the selling process.

CHAPTER 4

How to Find Allies

THE SEARCH FOR POTENTIAL ALLIES will be equally intuitive and data-driven. The objective is to identify people with whom you've had an association and determine their level of Mindset through the quantitative Categorization Equation, and sometimes through an educated guess. In each case, various databases should be reviewed, including all electronic lists, business card inventories, social media associates, and your own memory. The lists will provide a starting point to reenergize your memory and begin the evaluation process.

The first step will be to decide who has a Business-Development Mindset. The next step is to assign these potential Allies to one of the five Ally categories. The initial categorization will most likely change or be deleted as the interactions with these potential Allies begin. The final step will be to enlist the process to find new people with whom you've had no prior interaction.

Research Your Existing List of Entities

A. Personal Contacts

Create a working list from your inventory of Contacts, reviewing all databases, including your mental database—friends, colleagues, or any other individual with whom you've had a significant interaction. You can choose a handful of people with whom you've most recently been interacting with for a level of comfort and speed. Later, you can greatly expand the list to include those further back in your past, regardless of the length of time since that last interaction occurred. Although this may seem like a monumental task, you will find that the selection process will become second nature and you will be able to intuitively isolate productive Contacts.

B. Business Colleagues

Review and list your existing customers, coworkers, or any other entity that you encounter during business activities. The names can be placed immediately in the Process Ally category. Customers are and will always be **Permanent Process Allies**, and the rest will be **Transient Allies** until they are recategorized.

> **Permanent Process Allies:** your existing base of customers.
>
> **Transient Process Allies:** people encountered in the daily business process that will typically end up in another category.

C. The 7-Step Process

The 7-Step Process is designed to identify and engage new entities to build a database of Allies. The steps provide a framework for isolating potential Ally Opportunities and employing the techniques to identify those people possessing a Business-Development Mindset. The process is specifically designed for use in the Partner Ally category; however, since prospecting for new Partner Allies is the same as building a new database from scratch, the method works for both.

It is more a guide than a blueprint and is designed to initiate a network-building process. Basically, if you're starting out with a blank slate and don't know anyone in the world, then this would be the way to start. Of course, no one has a completely blank slate of Contacts, but if you're sitting alone in a new sales territory or a cubicle, the 7-Step Process would be the way to begin prospecting.

The 7-Step Process

Step 1: Identify a complementary industry.

Determine what other industries sell to the same type of decision-maker for your product or are a potential vertical industry for your product. The significance of this first step is that it presents a multitude of potential Allies because, within complementary industries, there will be a variety of people at all positions and levels. The position that the decision-maker holds determines how compatible the industry may be. For instance, if the decision-maker of an organization is the CFO, their array of product purchases is virtually everything the organization needs. The more specific the role of the individual, the narrower the potential products or people they will be associated with. However, these potential Allies can range from salespeople to finance executives to IT managers. The spectrum is limitless. As a Target decision-maker becomes more centralized in function, the Ally possibilities are reduced but still abundant. For example:

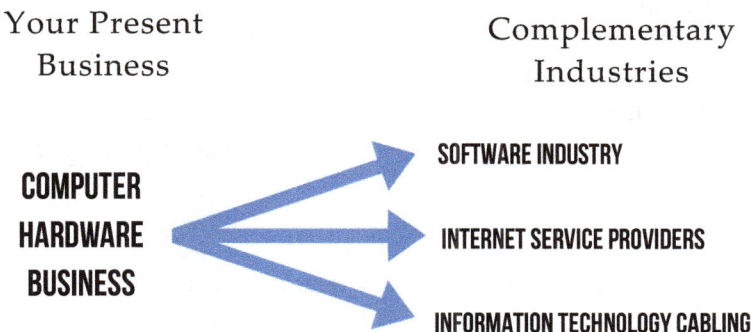

Your Present Business	Complementary Industries

COMPUTER HARDWARE BUSINESS

SOFTWARE INDUSTRY

INTERNET SERVICE PROVIDERS

INFORMATION TECHNOLOGY CABLING

While initiating Step 1 within the first hour of the first day of a new sales position, I reviewed with my manager the matching Target decision-maker for our product, which turned out to be an IT manager. As I was new to the geographic territory as well as the industry, I reviewed LinkedIn and isolated several IT consultants in the area. I knew that consultants would have their own base of IT managers with some type of relationship. I isolated these potential Allies that were in my territory.

The tactics would be to first choose IT consultants with matching Target decision-makers for my product. Then I would communicate with the consultant, set up a meeting, learn their business interests, and develop a plan that would benefit both of us. I reviewed a consultant's profile in-depth, then first chose the strongest personal associates. In this case, they were people who wrote recommendations for them on their profile page. This was a way to quickly select people with the strongest link through familiarity.

As it turned out, one of the recommendations for a certain IT consultant was written by a salesperson sitting two desks away from me. As a goodwill gesture, as well as to Anchor Seed, I printed out the information and placed it on her desk with a note describing that person as an excellent potential "networking partner." When the salesperson saw the note, she came over to me demanding to know how I found the consultant, as if I was doing something deceitful or read her mind. Because, in her perception, how else could I have discovered such a valuable Lead in the first thirty minutes of my first day?

The reason it was so valuable was that the consultant was her best friend. In her thinking, that was no coincidence. And since she couldn't follow my description of the Alliance Process, she wouldn't accept that explanation. It's not that she was concerned about losing a friend. Her real fear was losing the customers that her best friend was feeding her. These customers were of course portrayed by her as cold-calling successes. This is an example of a Sales Professional employing Tactical Prospecting without knowing it.

Step 2: Identify a complementary organization in that industry.

At this step, identify an organization with selling needs complementary to your own. The reason to Target organizations that can provide Allies rather than only hunting for people in the 7-Step Process is that it accomplishes two objectives. The first is that it provides a better chance of finding a Lead who sells a product to other Target decision-makers that are like your Target decision-makers. And second, the organization itself becomes a potential customer for your product, thereby removing all the prospecting obstacles—for example, two products that are both IT based but function differently, such as computer hardware and telephone systems:

1. Those products will both match similar Target customers to sell to, which in this case is extensive since virtually all companies use these products and vary only by size and possibly geographic selling regions.
2. They will have similar Target IT product decision-makers.

Your Present
Business

Chosen Complementary
Business

**COMPUTER
HARDWARE
BUSINESS**   ⟶   **COMPUTER
SOFTWARE
BUSINESS**

To be clear, you *should only* prospect organizations to locate potential Allies within them. You should *not* prospect organizations as end-user customers to sell. Your goal is to communicate with an organization to identify a person within it that possesses the same selling interests as your own. The secondary value of forming an Ally within the organization is to create an unencumbered route to selling to that organization directly.

Step 3: Identify a key person in the organization.
This can be any person at any level. However, if going in with limited knowledge of the employees there is a practical way of viewing this process. It makes sense that a sales employee at some level in the organization would be the appropriate person to

address. It could be someone at a senior level, middle management, or some type of field salesperson. I have had the most success with the field sales-level individuals because they are the most motivated to find new ways to generate Leads. For Example:

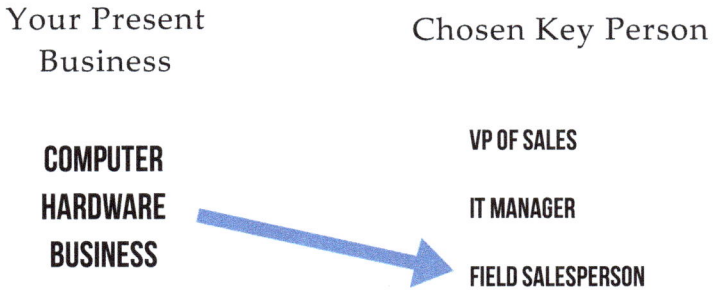

Your Present Business	Chosen Key Person
COMPUTER HARDWARE BUSINESS	**VP OF SALES**
	IT MANAGER
	FIELD SALESPERSON

Middle managers usually don't have the desire to upset the apple cart by trying something different. Also, there's a paranoia with sales managers. They're afraid of providing customer information to an outsider as well as introducing members of their sales team to a new organization, fearing that they will jump ship. Middle managers are also more likely to be wedded to company procedures, giving the impression that they're in complete control of their sales force regardless of whether those procedures yield any results.

Senior-level sales executives aren't as cooperative as field salespeople, but they are open to new prospecting methods. I don't want to speculate as to their motivation, except to say that it is easy for them to delegate a new idea and gauge the results without having to implement it themselves on a day-to-day basis. I would stay away from national sales managers and vice presidents of sales because they either don't have the time to meet, don't match many of the parameters, or—in my experience—are perfectly content living off the fat of the land. If there's enough fat.

I once pitched a satiated manager when I was a vice president. I set up a meeting with a new, large vendor to resell their product through our multiple sales channels. At the time, we had a tremendous network of distribution throughout the US. After a few minutes of pitching the strength of my distribution network to him, the owner of the company (who was in the meeting passively listening) could tell that the national sales manager couldn't care less about a single word coming out of my mouth.

The owner interrupted and said to him, "Can I ask you a question?"

He said, "Sure."

The owner asked, "It doesn't matter to you whether or not you get this account, does it?"

To my amazement, he replied, "Not to be disrespectful, but no, not really." He further explained, "You see it's like a bucket of water; the sales fill the bucket to a point. Then if more sales come in, it just overflows to a level where there's too many sales to handle. I'm at that point." I could not believe that I heard a Sales Professional use the phrase "too many sales" as a negative. The truth is that he didn't want to bring on another distributor because that might have alienated the others who were filling his bucket — the fat of the land.

Step 4: Organize the names.

Keep a list: Excel, black book, napkins, whatever is your preference. Okay, I'll be more helpful. Over the years I have had the "Burning of Alexandria" type of luck with information that I've entrusted to the electronic world. I can condense the information of a thousand books to a portable device one inch long. That's good. However, I also can't lose a thousand books unless I condense them into that same one-inch portable device. I've lost more valuable information to IT glitches, cheap devices, replaced hard drives—and probably my carelessness—in my career than should be allowed by that level of technology. So, I trust tactile information. I use binders with business-card holders as backup.

Contact List Business Card Database

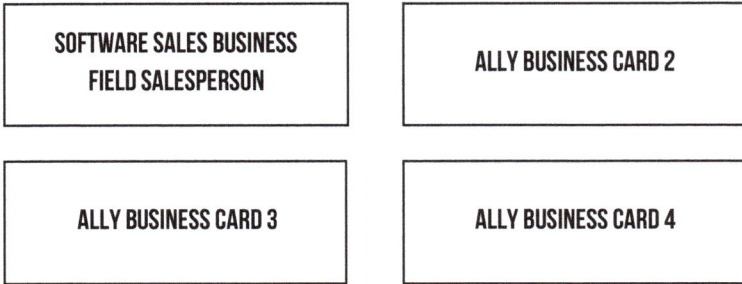

SOFTWARE SALES BUSINESS FIELD SALESPERSON	ALLY BUSINESS CARD 2
ALLY BUSINESS CARD 3	ALLY BUSINESS CARD 4

Step 5: Communicate and meet.

An initial meeting is required, and once you meet with the Lead, they become a Contact. The meeting does not have to be face to face, and it doesn't necessarily have to be based on an agreement to develop business, as long as that's what occurs. An example of an agreed-upon, business-development relationship is both parties agreeing to exchange Leads that match each other's Targets. Their future behavior will determine which category they will occupy.

Business-Development Agreement to Exchange Leads

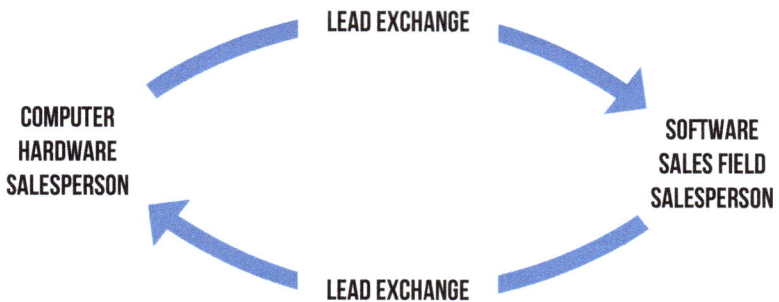

LEAD EXCHANGE

COMPUTER HARDWARE SALESPERSON

SOFTWARE SALES FIELD SALESPERSON

LEAD EXCHANGE

Step 6: Attend Networking Events

Attend all the events that are typically thought of as networking events with the focused intent of identifying the one or two people with the Mindset to become an Ally. Then categorize them. Don't mingle! If you're successful, the event will probably end for you in about an hour. For example:

Your Present
Business

Networking Event
Directory

**COMPUTER
HARDWARE
SALESPERSON**

ATTENDEE 1

ATTENDEE 2

ATTENDEE 3: IT MANAGER

ATTENDEE 4

Step 7: Recruit Point-of-Sale (POS) Allies

The POS Ally can be two things. It can be a business that resells your product as part of its normal distribution model: **a POS Reseller**. It can also be a business that sells your product as a new product that complements its product line and matches its Target customer: **a POS Partner**. There are two methods used to recruit a Point-of-Sale business entity. The first is to identify and negotiate with existing Point-of-Sale businesses that are established, normal distributors designed to resell your products in your industry. And the second is to create a new Point-of-Sale Ally that would not typically exist in the industry. This is done by identifying and negotiating with new distribution entities that sell products that are complementary to your main product. Although these POS Allies are not typical for reselling your product, the tactic is to make them new points of distribution through a mutually beneficial deal.

COMPUTER HARDWARE SALESPERSON

POS RESELLER

COMPUTER HARDWARE STORE

POS PARTNER

IT-MANAGED SERVICES BUSINESS

How to Categorize Allies

Passive Ally

Process Ally

Partner Ally

Party Ally

Point-of-Sale Ally

The Categorization Process begins by determining the Mindset strength of your Allies. The parameters used to match an Ally with the proper category are of paramount importance to the success of the process. I will describe in detail the features of each of the five categories and isolate their key characteristics. It is crucial to gain an understanding of each category, as effects on your time, effort, and interaction techniques vary based on the Ally category.

The categories are listed in order of least to most productive. Now, the productivity factor does not mean value; the categories are equally valuable and necessary, but some will have the ability to generate many more Leads on a continual basis in a specific time than others do. And knowing the differences allows you to utilize the Allies according to their specific Mindset attributes.

The key terms used throughout this section are **Contacts** and **Allies**. A Contact is a Lead with whom you've had some Significant Interaction. And a Significant Interaction is an interaction that starts or becomes a communication with business-development subject matter, even if the interaction didn't start out with that purpose. An Ally is a Contact with whom you've established an agreed-upon relationship that will facilitate continual interactions. This can be any type of relationship as long as it is mutually agreed-upon. Whether you meet on a regular basis for a business discussion or just to play golf, if the relationship is established and continual and the subject matter consists of productive business development, then the person is an Ally. Before we examine the Categorization Process, let's review a scenario of the progression of steps from Lead to Ally:

Lead: First, you identify consultants in your industry with access or some type of connection to your matching prospects' decision-makers.

Contact: After the meeting has taken place, if you've described to each other your ideal customer type, and there has been an exchange of business-development ideas or a Significant Interaction, then that Lead is now a Contact.

Ally: Finally, you both agree to meet again. This can be to meet a new Lead, to create a prospecting plan, or to exchange further information about potential customers. At this point, they're converted from a Contact to an Ally, and the Categorization Process begins.

From the initial identification to successfully forming the agreed-upon relationship, a singular person's status changes from Lead to Contact to Ally.

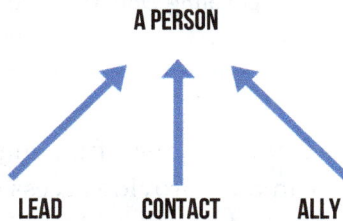

A PERSON

LEAD   CONTACT   ALLY

One final point concerning this description: the progression of steps reflects what's typical, not what's mandatory. The first step can be any of the listed components, and the subsequent steps can be in any order that possesses the features of that next component. The starting point is dependent only on the characteristics of the first encounter as created by the prospecting tactics you employ.

```
┌─────────────────────────────────────────────┐
│                    ALLY                       │
│                                               │
│   A person who possesses the characteristics  │
│   of a Target, a Lead, and a Contact and has  │
│   a mutually accepted existence of a          │
│   relationship with you.                      │
└─────────────────────────────────────────────┘
```

┌──────────────────────────┐   ┌──────────────────────────────────┐
│   TARGET   │   │   AGREED-UPON RELATIONSHIP   │
│   │   │   │
│   An entity that can   │   │   The mutually accepted exist-   │
│   provide any level of   │   │   ence of a relationship.   │
│   prospecting   │   │   │
│   productivity.   │   │   │
└──────────────────────────┘   └──────────────────────────────────┘

LEAD	SIGNIFICANT INTERACTION	CONTACT
A person who has access to a Target with which you've had no communication for the purposes of business development.	A communication with the purposes of business development in the form of identifying, engaging, or negotiating Opportunities.	A person who possesses the characteristics of a Lead with which you've had a communication for the purposes of business development.

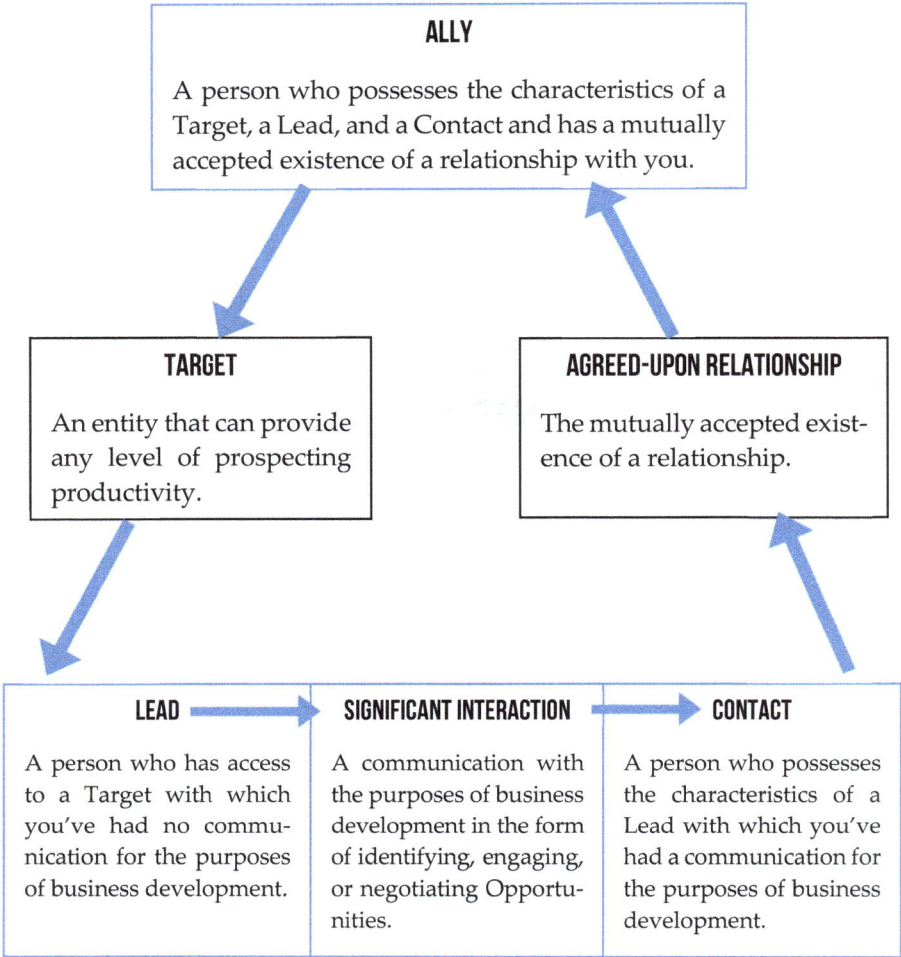

As shown in the diagram, you may first engage an Ally, who identifies a Target and can then provide access to the Target with a Lead. You then communicate—a Significant Interaction. Or you may enter a new industry and enlist an existing Contact, then agree to exchange Leads on a regular basis, thereby forming an Alliance. The progression of steps is dependent on using your tactical-prospecting ability to choose what is the best first step. And except when the first step is the Target, each component in the process contains all the characteristics of the previous components in the sequence.

The Five Categories

The categories are listed along the spectrum of two main attributes. First, they're placed in descending order from least to greatest Lead-generating ability or Mindset strength. Determining this ability allows for the proper category placement of the Ally and thus the appropriate interaction. The characteristics of the category never change, but the characteristics of the Ally may change. And second, they're listed from least to most difficult to establish as an Ally. The combination of the two attributes will determine which Allies should be engaged, how they should be interacted with, and what structure the relationship should take to produce the most in the least amount of time.

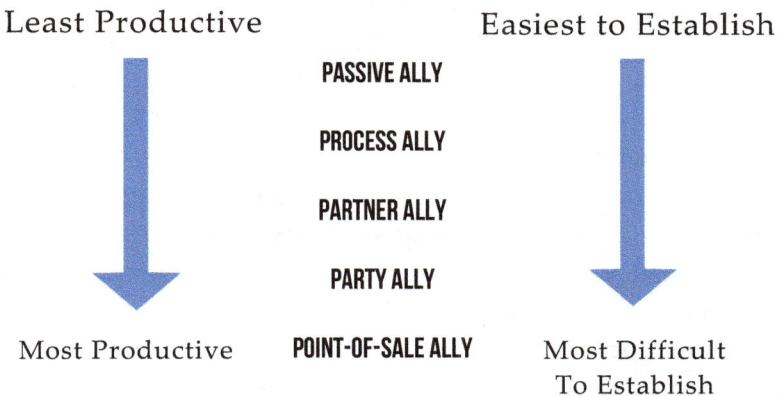

Least Productive		Easiest to Establish
	PASSIVE ALLY	
	PROCESS ALLY	
	PARTNER ALLY	
	PARTY ALLY	
Most Productive	**POINT-OF-SALE ALLY**	Most Difficult To Establish

1. Least-to-Most Lead-Generating Productivity

The deciding factor for the categorization of a person is pure and simple: the strength of their Business-Development Mindset. This may seem like a superficial description, but remember, sales requires talent. And some of these talents are the ability to identify people who provide productivity, their level of productivity, or their potential for productivity. These sales talents are initially used to make categorization decisions until a sufficient number of interactions occur to provide reliable data for the Categorization Equation.

1. Least-to-Most-Difficult to Establish

The ease or difficulty of establishing an Alliance relationship affects the investment of time. For instance, some Allies understand and actively seek to offer their Contacts as **Referrals** simply as a normal course of communication, while others not only don't understand business development but also raise an **Invisible Shield** when a business discussion is merely broached. That's why, as mentioned earlier, Tactical Prospecting requires the same abilities used in selling. With a reluctant customer, the sales techniques employed are by no means the same as with a customer who needs to purchase your product immediately. The same is true when dealing with Allies. You will determine the characteristics of the person and employ the appropriate techniques. When your Allies are properly categorized according to their Mindset, then you will know exactly how and when to interact with them.

> **Referral:** a person whose identity was provided by another person and who exerts some level of influence.
>
> **Invisible Shield:** a protection that prevents certain sales communication from entering the prospects' comfort zone as if they want to *defend* being "sold."

Category Impermanence

Allies can also change categories. They usually increase their productivity as the interactions increase; however, they can also regress into characteristics of less-productive categories. This will be discovered after analyzing the metrics from the Categorization Equation. Remember, we are dealing with human beings and all the traits they carry. They can become tired of the process, angered, have personal issues, or lack time. The reasons are endless and, on the surface, meaningless. The most important thing is that you recognize their Lead-productivity value, place them in the proper category, and move on. As categories change, the type of interactions must also be altered. It would be analogous to a customer account that decreased by half. You couldn't change that fact, and you also couldn't sell them the same volume or type of product as you did when they were twice as large. It would be a futile strategy, even if it was imposed on you.

The Categorization Equation

If you can't instinctively determine the existence or level of a person's Mindset, I have no intention of just leaving you to your wits, hoping that intuition would prevail. Eventually it will. But until then, let's allow metrics to prevail. To ensure that the proper Ally is assigned to the proper category, the Categorization Equation can be used to ascertain the person's Mindset. The basis of the equation relies on the three key elements used to determine an Ally's productivity value:

1. The Ally's raw number of Leads that have access to Targets and the Ally's power over the Targets.
2. The Ally's raw number of Opportunities they offer to you per month.
3. The Ally's raw number of monthly Significant Interactions you have with them.

Significant Interaction in Planning and Content

1. Significance by Planning

Significance by Planning basically means that the interaction was determined in advance. With Significance by Planning, a simple acid test is whether a scheduled "invite" was used to first set up the meeting for business development. If you have a planned meeting with an Ally for coffee for the purpose of business development, whether or not any business-development subject matter is discussed, that still qualifies as a planned Significant Interaction.

2. Significance by Content

Significance by Content means that it makes no difference how the meeting was established; what matters is the content of the interaction. If the meeting was spontaneous or by chance but it still discussed business-development information, then it was Significance by Content.

For metrics-recording purposes, if you meet by chance and spend an hour with that same Ally and attempt to change the subject to business development, that will count as a Significant Interaction whether you succeed or fail. If you meet by chance at the local coffee shop and talk about your kids, that doesn't qualify as a measurable Significant Interaction.

What is most important is that the Significant Interaction, whether planned or by content, can be used only as data in the equation with an established Ally. If you meet a person by chance who is not presently an Ally and proceed to discuss business-development interactions prior to any agreed-upon relationship, at that point that person would be a Contact. Metrics used in the equation are derived from Significant Interactions with existing Allies for the sole purpose of categorization. The object of the equation is to calculate how often something productive is gained from an interaction with an Ally in order to derive a categorization index value.

The Components of the Equation

1	Access Ranking
2	Monthly Opportunities
3	Monthly Interactions
4	Category Grid
5	Category Index

The equation reads:

$$\text{(ACCESS RANKING} \times \text{MONTHLY OPPORTUNITIES)} - \text{MONTHLY INTERACTIONS} = \text{CATEGORY INDEX}$$

The calculation provides an index value to determine the category placement of an Ally. The Access Ranking of the Ally is multiplied by the Monthly Opportunities to provide a weighted value. The number of interactions is then deducted from this weighted value to determine a productivity Category Index and its corresponding category. The equation is designed to calculate the amount of time invested with a particular Ally and the resulting value of any gained Opportunities. Think of it as simply answering the question, "What am I gaining by communicating with this Ally?"

1. Access Ranking

The Access Ranking is a power-index ranking applied to the Ally. It represents the influence they would have over their Contacts. For instance, CEOs would presumably provide more engagement influence over their own key people as opposed to a lower-level manager or rank-and-file employee.

Access Power Rankings Table

The ranking levels have quantitative values as they relate to each other:

INDIVIDUAL ENTITY RANKING		BUSINESS ENTITY RANKING	
Non-Sales Professional	1	Customer Base 1–100	6
Sales Professional	2	Customer Base 101–250	7
Middle Management	3	Customer Base 251–500	8
Senior Management	4	Customer Base 501–1,000	9
Owner/CEO	5	Customer Base 1,000 +	10

The two distinct ranking lists are separated according to the Ally type: Individual Entity or Business Entity. An Individual Entity is given an Access power ranking based on their professional position. Any individuals who don't have one of the listed professions would be a miscellaneous, or Non-Sales Professional.

A Business Entity is an operating business and is ranked according to the size of its customer base, which in our world are Targets and potential Contacts. The Customer Base ranking is an Access power level associated with the range and influence that particular Ally type would have over these Targets. The Business Entity typically starts out as a Process Ally because it's either an existing customer or a prospected customer. It remains a Process Ally until the point when their Category Index number increases, and they are recategorized.

2. Monthly Opportunities

The Monthly Opportunities are defined by the level of availability offered to establish the quickest agreed-upon relationships. The availability is the means to create some form of communication connection between the parties. It can be a formal meeting to focus on identifying Leads, a weekly business coffee meeting, or as simple as a round of golf. Business-development productivity can take the form of simply providing Leads or it can be the potential sale itself. These Opportunities can't be in name only; the Leads must produce results.

3. Monthly Interactions

Monthly Interactions are a total number of communications intended for business development between you and the Ally that occur in a single month. Since the interactions are with existing Allies, the only requirement is that they are agreed upon, and they don't necessarily have to be a typical business-oriented environment. If you play golf once a week with a sales manager, then that is an agreed-upon interaction. If you attend a weekly coffee meeting with a potential Ally, that is also an agreed-upon interaction. If you wait in the parking lot next to a VP's parking space every Friday to test your elevator pitch and fail, that may be a recurring interaction, but it is in no way agreed upon. It might, however, be a prospecting technique offered in a different sales-training class. The Monthly Interactions are the most important element in the equation to determine the productivity Mindset and, hence, the category of the Ally. The agreed-upon relationship is a vehicle to remove any communication obstacles that can provide for a free flow of Significant Interactions. When parties can meet to talk or email or communicate freely, then the situation is already in place. There are no preliminary introduction hurdles, and you can move right into discussing Opportunities.

Disregarding for a moment the Access or Access Ranking of the Ally, calculating the number of Opportunities per Interaction would, by itself, provide immediate insight into the characteristics of an Ally. If I met with an Ally twice a week or eight times a month and received one Opportunity, then the Interactions to Opportunities would be a negative number:

1 OPPORTUNITY OFFERED - 8 INTERACTIONS PER MONTH = -7 CATEGORY INDEX

4. Category Grid

The Category Grid is a chart used to segment the Ally by category. As you can see in the graph below, the categories are separated by sectors. Using the equation to calculate the category index, you can easily determine in which sector to place the Ally. The highest and lowest metric on the y-axis of thirty relates to a thirty-day month. For practical purposes of analysis, anticipate that only one Interaction can take place per day or thirty in a month.

Data Examples:

ALLY	ACCESS RANK		MONTHLY OPPORTUNITIES		MONTHLY INTERACTIONS		CATEGORY INDEX
Sales Professional	2	×	6	-	4	=	8
CEO	5	×	0	-	2	=	-2
Existing Account 0–100	6	×	1	-	1	=	5
Non-Sales Professional	1	×	0	-	10	=	-10

Category Placement Grid

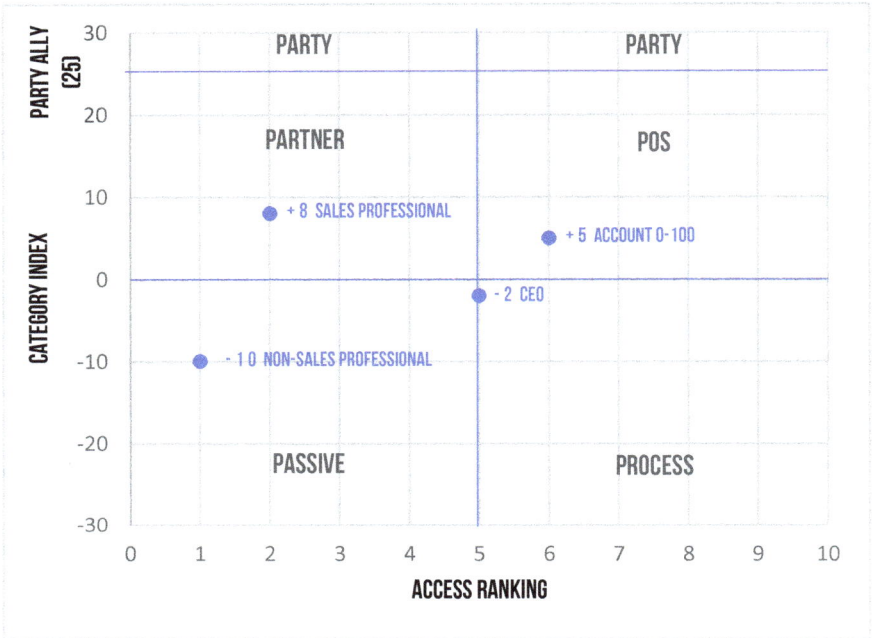

Party Ally Sectors

The Party Ally Sectors in the upper portion of the graph are the very specific areas used to determine which Allies should be advanced to the next level and used in the Party Ally Method. These Allies are the jewels of the Tactical Prospecting world. This sector of the graph is the most-productive index level and includes those people that produce the most Opportunities with the least amount of time invested. If an Ally in one category has a high index value, it won't necessarily have a high productive value as a Party Ally. And if the Party Ally Method is chosen but you haven't yet acquired any Allies that reach that level, then select the Allies with the next highest Category Index.

PART THREE

Ally Categories:
The Upside-Down Funnels

PASSIVE	PROCESS	PARTNER	PARTY	POINT-OF-SALE
		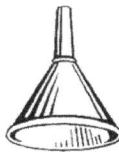		

AFTER SEGMENTING THE LIST of Allies by category sector, transfer the names to each category in a list according to their characteristic Mindset Index. Remember that they can, and will, change categories after further Interactions. The Process Ally column will be disproportionately longer than the other columns due to the greater number of people whom you encounter in business on a day-to-day basis. Also, a portion of them will initially be categorized as Transient Process Allies, which means a list will begin temporarily longer until you can fully determine characteristics and recategorize.

CHAPTER 5

The Passive Ally

"The One-Shot Deal"

A PASSIVE ALLY IS an agreed-upon relationship with a person that's the easiest to establish and the least productive in terms of raw number of Leads generated. Such a person has the weakest Mindset for business development and seldom realizes they're an Ally in the first place. As a result, they don't feel an obligation or desire to be actively developing business. They do, however, have access to valued Targets. Although they produce the fewest number of total Leads of any Ally, the Leads that are generated are no less powerful than any Leads produced by the other categories. This is a very important point to be aware of because it defines the main characteristic when dealing with a Passive Ally — that is, they're a "one-shot deal." What that means is they'll be able to provide only Tactical Prospecting assistance once, usually at the very beginning or the very end of a targeted-prospect engagement. After that, they don't have the ability to provide any more Leads.

At the Beginning of the Sale

Most often a Passive Ally is employed at the beginning of a selling engagement. They will be used to provide access to an influential person who'll assist with penetrating the organization and getting the ball rolling. In most cases, the reason a Passive Ally relationship is formed is because the Passive Ally has access to an entity that you determine will be a Target at a later date. The Ally's access to a valuable Target is determined first, and the Ally is then created. Pursuit of the Target is attempted at a later time when the Target matches the product you're selling. This may seem backward, but Passive Allies are formed and warehoused because of their access to Targets. The formation of the Passive Alliance may not be immediate, and often this Ally isn't a matching Target for the product you're presently selling, but it will be eventually.

At the End to Seal the Deal

Conversely, at the end of a selling engagement, when going for the close, you can use a Passive Ally for access to an influential person within the organization to help seal the deal. It's in this situation that the concept of the one-shot deal really comes into play. In your mind, you are engaging them in a Tactical Prospecting activity, and in their mind, they are merely helping you as an acquaintance. That brings me to a secretly sinister, yet useful, point: much of the time during the Alliance Process, Passive Allies don't really know that they're Allies and that they're providing a service within a formalized process.

Engaging Allies on a repeated basis is the regular activity associated with the other categories. But to a Passive Ally, helping an acquaintance on a repeated basis becomes an annoyance. Therefore, you won't be able to go to them for their Contact engagement more than once. They should be viewed as the "ace in the hole," because after that, their ability to help, desire to help, and patience to help will be exhausted. We don't need to know why; we just need to know that it is.

One exception is if the Passive Ally changes roles in some way—maybe gets promoted or moves to a new organization. At that point, their new value as an Ally can potentially be re-energized. However, even if this change occurs, and they don't develop the characteristics of the other Ally types, they will still be Passive with a new one-shot deal. You may be questioning why this is important to know. The answer relates to the most important asset needed when prospecting: time. After categorizing a Contact as a new Passive Ally and being provided the *one shot*, any further engagement time would be a waste.

Finding Passive Allies

The steps involved in identifying a Passive Ally are exploratory. You must be attentive to people you find or are made aware of and log them both physically and mentally. Finding Allies starts simply by looking for them. They can be initially encountered in multiple ways. They can be hunted, located by chance, transferred to this category from the Process Ally category, and, quite often, encountered on a personal basis. You may be wondering why Passive Allies are not formed utilizing the 7-Step Process for identifying Allies. That goes back to the Mindset requirement. A Contact with a poor Mindset will not consciously move to form an Alliance. So, what you are left with is meeting people through the methods just described or through your daily business processes. Then you place them in the Passive Ally category because they have access to a Target before you can pursue the Target. They are also available through common methods of interaction such as socializing, electronic databases, lists of personal acquaintances, colleagues, or even gossip. The objective of reviewing any of these sources is to facilitate an interaction, whether proactively or through happenstance. The key is to identify the strength of their access to a Target. Since they are already in your database of Contacts, presumably a significant communication has been made. The next step is to form an agreed-upon relationship. With Passive Allies, the relationships are typically more social and thus provide both amiability and availability.

Proactive Passive Ally for Future Productivity

The proactive nature of a Passive Ally is the most important point in the identification process. The Target does not have to be one that you're pursuing at present, in which case the Passive Ally's Lead-developing strength increases its business-development strength. What makes a Passive Ally a quality Ally is its access to a valuable Target that can be pursued in the future.

Due to access, I interacted for years with a Passive Ally, who was a CEO of a building supplies company. I had met the Ally several years earlier when he was the general manager and determined his category. After several interactions, the relationship produced a net negative business-Opportunity index. I then categorized him as a Passive Ally in my physical and mental database, knowing it would take an extremely specific product match to engage him or his Contacts for a sale.

By the way, these matching characteristics that ignite the *one shot* can really be anything of value, such as another Target Contact, Target piece of information, Target Opportunity for one of your other Allies—it doesn't really matter. All that matters is the value because that translates into your time.

Several years passed, and he ultimately took over the position of CEO. At that time, I was working in sales, developing a channel for a product that specifically matched his company. I invited him out for coffee and used Misdirection by discussing other potential Referrals he may have for me, but all the time I knew who my real Target was—him.

I wouldn't necessarily use Misdirection for stronger Mindset category Allies, but in this case, it was the appropriate selling technique.

Now was the time to discuss the product, discuss the value, and most importantly, discuss the Target customer. As expected, he offered his own organization as a matching customer without my having to ask. The six-month sales cycle that was typical for this product was reduced to two weeks. And then I moved on to the next sale.

One point to mention: I've closed many other sales with a

similar process; however, when I showed Management how quickly it was completed, thereby decimating the sales cycle, the most frequent response was, "That's only because you knew him." Exactly!

Retroactive Passive Ally for Present Productivity

I created a cumbersome title for this method, so hopefully you won't have to use it. But it does need to be discussed. The Retroactive Passive Ally is the technique of searching for an influential person with access to your Target after you've prospected an organization as the first step, instead of first identifying an Ally with access to it. The process is more limiting because you're pursuing a singular Target, such as a singular business to sell to.

*A sore reminder of this was when I was having a difficult time trying to get a response from a project manager of a multinational construction company in order to sell our subcontract services to them for a very specific project. Our services were perfect for that portion of the construction project if I could simply establish a line of communication with him. I prospected the company for a month, and with some basic research, I retroactively identified a person in the accounting department that had a relationship with one of my Contacts. He was more than willing to assist and was able to hand my proposal directly to the project manager. This was done. However, thinking it was a slam dunk for me, after a month of follow-up communications, I learned that the project manager got reassigned and was no longer in charge of that project for some time. No one was aware of that. As I scrambled to beat the proposal deadline, no one in the local office knew who took his place. I was sent on a networking wild-goose chase for days that ultimately produced just that: a **goose egg**.*

> **Goose Egg:** zero sales.

To overcome the limitations of this situation, the search for a Passive Ally will have to be expanded to include any person at all, with any access, at any level to the Target. It can be direct access by finding someone immediately connected to the Target, or indirect access by identifying a person further removed from the Target. The limitations can also be reduced by engaging multiple key people, thereby increasing the chances of reaching the decision-maker. The Retroactive Passive Ally should be used only as a last resort and is really the necessary evil caused by pursuing an individual organization first. It's more of an attempt to salvage a poorly prospected organization. As the Tactical Prospecting methodology is based on hunting for people, and these people provide Leads, engaging a Passive Ally retroactively can run dangerously close to cold calling and time wasting.

Remember, you have only one shot, so the time to broach the productivity topic with a Passive Ally is when you have already decided who the exact Target is and to whom they have access. This points the Ally in a direction you've decided to go and doesn't depend on their taking you to the right place.

In either case, the Proactive and Retroactive approach is designed to initiate or finalize the selling process with a potential customer. Due to the weaker Mindset of this category, when the one-shot is taken, quite often Misdirection must be employed. Their Mindset characteristics are not strong enough to allow them to freely engage in a productive exchange of Leads or even respond to a direct request for a Referral. Asking a Passive Ally for a Referral is as futile as demanding one from them. It will be interpreted by them as the same thing. And remember, the "why" doesn't matter.

Determine Their Value in the Sales Process

After determining the ability to sell a Passive Ally's Target, you must now determine the Ally's place in the selling process. You must decide how they can offer value with the Lead they have at their disposal and, most importantly, how to interact with them to gain access to their database of people. Passive Allies start out as a type of inventory warehouse of Leads that are added to your database to be used later, or to be used immediately for a very specific purpose that you determine.

Personal Friends

You cannot determine whether a friend is useful for your Tactical Prospecting until you know their Mindset characteristics. Personal acquaintances can become very powerful Allies even if they don't appear to be when first encountered. I've found friendships that begin in a social setting often maintain the roles formed in that environment. And they're difficult to transition into a business relationship while still in that setting. That's not to say that you can't have a business discussion, but it's like crossing a line. For example, think about the opposite: think of your best customer that you've had a great working relationship with for years but have only ever met with at their business office. It may seem out of place to impulsively invite that person to your home for dinner.

A Passive Warning

The danger with Passive Allies is a recurring belief that they possess more Lead-generating power than they actually do. It happens often, but the key is to determine this as soon as possible. And once their level of power has been decided, stick to your decision. There are techniques discussed later that can help determine the production value of a Contact before they are pursued as an Ally. Allies are what they are. You can't change them or make them more productive or force them into a different category through belief. Whether they can generate many Leads for you or are a one-shot deal can change. But you can't expect them to change by themselves nor can you change them yourself. Just use your talents of observation and deduction that all Sales Professionals possess. Identify when they change, then recategorize them accordingly. All Allies have value; the differences in the value are in their Lead-generating capabilities as it relates to your time invested. As you'll see, a Partner Ally has higher Lead-generating value than a Passive Ally in terms of pure gross number of Leads. And if you have them properly categorized, then the time allotment will be equally weighted.

Finally, the value of an Ally is in no way represented by their level in an organization. The only exception to this occurs when comparing Allies from the same category. For instance, a CEO that is a Passive Ally isn't more valuable than a sales representative that's a Partner Ally purely because of the C-level position. But the same CEO is more valuable than a lower-level employee if both are Passive Allies. The CEO's one-shot-deal offering has the potential of greater payoff.

An Aggressive-Passive Warning

Just as one of the components of Tactical Prospecting is identifying the productively level of each Contact prior to their becoming Allies, it is equally important to identify those individuals that believe they are quality Allies. They really want to be quality Allies but are nothing other than unproductive acquaintances that proactively waste your time. Imagine a person who can waste the time that you haven't even offered to them. Like a lifeguard tossing you a life preserver made of stone, these people will repeatedly provide low-quality information at best, and cold-calling advice at worst. The quality of their Opportunities is fraught with negative characteristics, from poor purchasing ability to being a poor Target match. They are basically substituting quantity as quality because they literally have less than zero understanding of Tactical Prospecting. If someone says, "I know plenty of people . . ." Well, who doesn't? Walking upright or breathing doesn't make a quality Lead. And the worst, as well as probably the most, insulting thing is when requesting Referrals is interpreted as requesting selling advice. But what is provided is cold-calling advice.

I encountered one of these advisors when I worked as a consultant selling a product that perfectly matched building contractors. By chance, I crossed paths with an old acquaintance who, as Opportunity would have it, was a building contractor. After introductions, I briefly described the product and asked him for other specific *names of building contractors that he knew personally, as a way of immediately gaining unencumbered introductions. Here it comes: interpreting that I was asking for prospecting advice, he said to me, "You know what you should do? Go to the phonebook and look under 'B' for building contractors, there's a ton of them . . ." Again, I can appreciate his limited understanding of sales and prospecting, but really, I'm a sales consultant; did he think I couldn't figure out to look in the phonebook? Let me make the futility of that statement even more apparent. Imagine in his contracting business, he needed to hire salespeople. So, he bumps into me on the street and asks, "Do you know any good salespeople I can call?" And I respond, "You know what you should do, go to the phonebook and look under 'S.'"*

Fortunately, there are whale-sized key indicators that will alert you to the danger of these nuggets of useless information. Some of them are phrases such as "Go to the phonebook," "Google it," "There's a networking group," "Join the Chamber of Commerce," "Hand out flyers." You've got to be kidding! If you request Referrals from a person for Leads, and their response is "hand out flyers," your next action should be to thank them, then run for the hills. On second thought, don't even thank them, just run. They'll think you're eager to test their advice. I've experienced this. They later tell all their friends how they had to teach me to sell.

As you become more and more proficient at Tactical Prospecting, the ability to identify meaningful and meaningless information will become second nature, in which case, these people will probably remain Leads but can never become Allies.

CHAPTER 6

The Process Ally

"Get Referrals!"

A PROCESS ALLY IS an agreed-upon relationship established with a person whom you encountered during your daily business processes. Think of it as a nine-to-five-business Ally. The Process Ally is more difficult to establish than a Passive Ally but will produce a higher level of productivity in terms of the raw number of Leads. The main principle of the Process Ally is an automatic familiarity and an automatic interaction produced by people becoming immediate colleagues in the same business environment. Whether the association is formed from being coworkers or from interacting at any level with a business associate, the relationship is initially spontaneous. Since the relationship is implied as colleagues of the organization, it requires less effort than the preceding category. Also, because you are connected in the same business environment, the familiarity is also implied, and this removes the Invisible Shield.

Although the difficulty of establishing a Process Ally is greater than that of a Passive Ally, it's still the quickest "bang for the buck" for a new Sales Professional. It provides quick prospecting traction and often quick sales. One unique characteristic of the Process Ally is that they offer a wellspring of their own colleagues and acquaintances to be accessed once their characteristics are identified and a relationship is established. If you think about people whom you encounter in your daily course of business, or even more accurately, that you have access to during your daily course of business, you will quickly realize what I mean. Calculating the number of people with whom you interact with during a business day, then the number of the people that they are associated with in all aspects of their life, you can see that the list grows exponentially. All that is left is determining the best way to interact with them. This is where the creativity of selling comes into play.

Again, the productivity level of each Ally is determined by the pure number of continual Leads generated. One reason for the increased difficulty in interacting with the Process Ally is the high level of divergent Mindset characteristics within the enclosed environment of a workplace. Coworkers, managers, executives, vendors, and potential and existing customers will have varying levels of Business-Development Mindsets. As these Mindsets are identified, you'll have to recategorize them into different Ally categories before pursuing an Alliance relationship. If they're not initially recategorized, this will create a greater possibility of attributing to them Mindset characteristics that don't really exist. To avoid this potentially confusing dynamic, there are two subsets of the Process Ally category to help you easily separate the real Ally type from the perceived one.

Transient Process Ally

The Transient Process Allies are people encountered in the daily business process who will typically end up in another category. The term *transient* doesn't imply a weakness or lack of ability to Tactically Prospect; on the contrary, they may potentially possess the strongest Mindset and ultimately be placed in a strong Mindset category. To explore the nature of these Allies, I have listed three common types of colleagues encountered in the business work environment.

Vendors

The main relationship value with a company's existing vendors is gaining access to their customers. However, there is also a much less obvious but much more productive synergy that can be formed. An informal business relationship can be created in which both parties can gain new business by "sharing the cost." The Sharing-the-Cost Mechanism will be expanded on later in the book.

Coworkers

It is often the case that coworkers come from companies in the same vertical industry as the new company. The coworker is hired because of their familiarity with the industry, with the product, or their relationship with an existing employee who may have had the same path into the organization. The colleagues from the previous organizations are the direct associates of these coworkers and direct Leads for you.

Supervisors

That's right, your boss is a Process Ally. How many prospects have salespeople received from their sales managers simply by being in their presence or through favoritism? It may sound ridiculous, but being a favorite is a technique of Tactical Prospecting because you can be fed prospects with little time invested.

A quick story that exemplifies the idea mentioned earlier. Salespeople can engage in Tactical Prospecting without even knowing it.

When I began a business-development position with a new company, it was the start of the baseball season. I was meeting with the vice president of sales at 11:00 a.m. when we were interrupted by the top sales producer in the company. And when I say "top," I mean he outproduced the second-best salesperson by 400 percent, and the typical account executive by 4,000 percent. Management fed him all the hot, multi-unit deals for reasons that don't really matter. He asked the VP of sales if he would allow any of his salespeople, the ones with 1/40th the production, to accompany him to the local sports bar and watch the baseball game because he didn't want to drink alone. The top producer could afford to miss the entire workday, without concern about lost productivity, and still outperform everyone in the company by a mile.

Unfortunately, favoritism as a Tactical Prospecting method is a "do or die" proposition. In the past, I often witnessed and wondered why the top-producing Sales Professionals in an organization had the most free time during the day, while the average Sales Professionals, or the ones having a bad month and producing little, were working their tails off, time-wise. I by no means make judgments about this behavior; on the contrary, I use it to reinforce my whole premise. The top-producing Sales Professionals have some significant advantage that relates to the Tactical Prospecting characteristics I am describing. Even if a salesperson is being "fed" by his manager and making President's Club each year, that is also Tactical Prospecting. In that case, the manager is a Process Ally regardless of what the relationship is based on.

And free time isn't the only advantage. Some do work awfully hard; however, their efforts produce a much greater result than any other Sales Professional working just as hard. The problem occurs when that relationship is dangled like a carrot and based on a ludicrous strategy. That being, if the Sales Professional is willing to perform wasted activity for months or years, then they'll earn the privilege to be fed. Even worse is when the top producers are enlisted by supervisors to tutor the low producers and they instruct them to engage in the common, useless prospecting methods that they'd never perform themselves. It's possible that if they also were fed potential deals, certain Sales Professionals would still fail at selling the same number of deals as the top producers. But that's no excuse. In that case, their sales managers can assist until they become more proficient. After that, if no positive change occurs then you know specifically that the failure is due to some factor other than prospecting.

And the ultimate tyranny in all of this is that sometimes these self-exalted tutors don't deny that they're being fed; they believe they deserve to be.

Let's take a different view of the situation. If the sales manager fed prospects to the entry-level Sales Professionals equally, it would accomplish three things:

1. It would provide a faster ascent to earning money, which motivates the professionals and reduces costly turnover.

2. It provides a faster development of the territory, which helps to fend off competition and reestablish market awareness—in essence, free marketing.

3. Lastly, and most importantly, it allows the tenured Sales Professional to efficiently address the *entire* volume of prospects available in their database. Allow me to expand on this one.

I worked at an organization where this strategy was so perverse that the top-producing Sales Professional sold ten times the dollar amount of revenue per year more than the top-untenured Sales Professional. Was he ten times better at selling than the others? No, the difference was that he had ten times the database of existing business, consisting of raw volume of prospects, as well as ten times the revenue-buying power of those prospects. He was also being fed the new prospects with similar parameters.

I was once suffering mightily from this situation. So, as a last-ditch effort to survive, I put together a report for my supervisor, trying to reason with him in a desperate attempt to earn more money. I recommended one minor adjustment that would increase the sales revenue by 33 percent per month, immediately. In my view, that would benefit me and the company, with no detrimental effect to anyone. As I explained, in this scenario only five accounts could realistically be sold in a month. Therefore, even if five hundred out of one thousand prospects were redistributed from the tenured salesperson, which left him with five hundred, he would still only sell five. It didn't matter if he had five hundred or seven hundred or one thousand in his database.

In this organization, the ten salespeople who were fed had a tenure of approximately ten years each, and the other twenty who were prospecting the old-fashioned way had a 100 percent turnover rate.

This was expressed in an annual-sales kickoff meeting when each of the twelve untenured members of the sales team had to present a sales plan for the upcoming year. By the end of that year, not a single presenter was still employed at the company, except for me. The entire sales team was turned over. The only reason I survived was that I negotiated a guaranteed commission payment for the first year. A decision I made after calculating my earnings potential with the Prospecting Productivity Equation when I was hired. Ironically, no one mentioned in their plan that an objective for the upcoming year was finding another job.

A Process Ally will produce various types of interactions — some friendly meetings, some authoritarian, some impromptu. They will require varying types of selling communication to establish the relationship. The Mindset of a vendor who is encountered infrequently may have the same Mindset level as an employee or an existing customer. However, the employee or the existing customer will have the advantage of familiarity and proximity, and as a result, have more productivity potential than the vendor. For example, the company's health insurance representative would have other Contacts at different companies in different industries that could use your product, but you may only have the one impromptu chance per year of interacting with that person face to face. Whereas a coworker will have the advantage of proximity, working in the same office, and can provide a more-productive referral-building relationship.

Permanent Process Ally

Permanent Process Allies are the existing base of customers. Their status as customers is the only determining factor that makes them a Permanent Ally. Of course, their permanence is only as long as they remain customers and consequently remain in this category. An existing customer can offer multiple Opportunities, assuming they have been a satisfied customer for some time. The most-productive Ally activity would be to purchase additional products, thereby providing a new Sales Professional with that quick sale I mentioned earlier. In this instance, the customer can be viewed as their own Referral because they are basically referring themselves as a purchaser. Talk about avoiding prospecting obstacles! They can also offer individual Referrals from their own database of people, both business and personal, with the potential of ultimately becoming one of the other Ally types.

The first step in identifying these Opportunities is to analyze your database of existing customers. Remember, when prospecting we are looking for the most Leads in the least amount of time. For this reason, existing customers are extremely valuable because they offer multiple Opportunities. For instance:

1. Referrals

By my definition, a Referral is a person whose identity was provided by another person and who exerts some level of influence. The influence by the referring party means that they have some effect on the person being referred. That effect can be authoritative, addressing a need, or simply providing familiarity. There are others as well, but regardless, the influence must exist because that is the mechanism to bypass prospecting obstacles. If there isn't some type of influence, then the offer is just a dressed-up cold call. And when dealing with Process Allies, particularly existing accounts, the Sales Professional must treat the process the same way as if they were selling them a product.

Gaining referrals from an Ally's network of contacts requires the same techniques used in selling. As a matter of fact, the reason most Sales Professionals fail at gaining Referrals is that they don't understand the nature of a referral and don't truly believe in this type of prospecting. As a result, they don't employ selling methods to obtain referrals. When Sales Professionals are instructed to get Referrals, the most frequently used talk track I have heard is, "Do you know anyone else who I could call (who may be interested in my product)?" And the customer will always reply, "No." Really? A person in the business world doesn't know a single human being who could possibly use your product. Of course they do. It was simply posed to them in a closed-ended manner, and they had neither the time nor inclination to think about it. I will show the weakness of that approach and it will be so glaringly obvious that I can then move on. For an entry-level Sales Professional—entry level in both the profession and the territory—Referrals really are the sale because they are building a territory from nothing. Now, apply that previous statement to a scenario of a sales call. Would the initial question to a prospect ever be, "Hello, do you want to buy my product?" That introductory question on a sales call would be ridiculous. There would first be consultation; probing; identification; my favorite, Misdirection; and closing.

There are several information sources that could be reviewed. You could find out about their business and associated people within that vertical, identify sources of those people, use social-networking databases, access customer lists, or even consult the accumulated business cards. Next, identify strong matches, probe further to learn more about them, and then request a meeting, with their permission. This may seem to be an unnecessarily lengthy process, but much of what has been described can also be accomplished in a face-to-face discussion. And comparing the success rate and closing ratio with that of the more time-consuming cold calling, the time investment is a drop in the bucket.

Therefore, what is crucial is to help them help you. Unfortunately, the main obstacle inhibiting the Referral process is the Sales Professional themselves. They don't consider gaining Referrals to be an important enough behavior to properly learn, or at least properly make the effort. And it does take effort, initially anyway. You must use the information gathered from some level of probing to identify these potential people and *you* suggest to them that these people may be a good customer for the product. Nobody knows anyone until you remind them, and you can't do that until you learn whom they know. It is your job to research their network of people ahead of time.

There are, of course, many creative ways to maneuver through this process as discussed earlier. The most powerful is to Anchor Seed by offering Leads to them first, and the **Counterweighing** is

> **Counterweigh:** gaining Leads from an Ally in return for providing Leads first.

usually immediate if they have the Mindset. Again, this may appear to be very labor-intensive, and it truly does take some time, but it is worth it. And for the skeptics, all I can say is that if you live by the sales metrics, you must die by the sales metrics. So, here are some metrics. Let's assume this process takes one hour and I gain three Referral Leads. That type of Referral typically has a 40 percent success rate for setting an appointment, and I gain that one appointment. To do the same cold calling, I would have to make one hundred calls, which would take all day and would not have nearly the quality of a Referral appointment. Remember, familiarity breeds comfort, so that Referral appointment would have a better closing ratio and very good potential of generating its own Referrals. A cold call is called *cold* for a reason.

On an appointment with a salesperson, I explained to him the importance of gaining Referrals. As I was about to walk him through the steps, he cut me off and said that he never asks for Referrals until he's sure that the customer is satisfied with the product. I replied, "How long do you wait?"

He said, ". . . Maybe six months."

I replied, "But what if the customer is satisfied after two months? You've lost four months waiting." Then he tried to rationalize the timeframe with some cockeyed logic. The probable truth was he didn't feel comfortable asking for Referrals and didn't want that revealed to me. But that would have been okay. As you will see, I would have helped anyway.

After the sales call was completed, which was really an account administrative call because the sale had already closed, I decided to literally teach the salesperson a lesson. The follow-up after the sale has closed is the perfect time to gain Referrals, and luckily for me, the owner was extremely cooperative. But do you know why? Because we were providing a unique service that he desperately needed to do more business. That's a lay down in the Referral world.

At the end of the meeting, I requested the Referrals, and the owner said, "Wait a moment." He left the room for a short period, and we heard a printer running for a few minutes. He then emerged with a four-inch-thick printout of his active customer base and told me to call them, that they needed this service too, and to use his name. Now, as he was their vendor, an introduction would be seamless because they needed each other's service and they'd be open to a meeting. And, in addition to the benefit of their relationship as a door opener, a vendor-client relationship also opened the door for many three-way, revenue-sharing Opportunities. While I was carrying the list, we walked back to the car. I said nothing. His silence was pleasantly apparent. As we settled back into the car and clicked our seatbelts, the Sales Professional finally broke the silence.

"Let me have that."

I said, "Have what?"

He said, "My list of Referrals."

I replied, "This is my list of Referrals. Your list won't be ready for six months."

With possession of a list of some three hundred clients and the potential business-development Opportunities that could have been created, a Sales Professional could have generated one year's worth of sales. And to accomplish this, all I did was go into the meeting with intent.

2. Add-On Sale

The best customer gained from a Referral is the customer themselves. And that's what an Add-On sale is—selling additional product to an existing customer. Simply put, they have referred themselves.

CHAPTER 7

The Partner Ally

"You Know Who You Should Call"

THE PARTNER ALLY IS an agreed-upon relationship established with a person who has the most-productive, Lead-generating ability in relation to the ease of establishing the relationship with them. They're extremely powerful Allies because of their instinctive Mindset for identifying business-development Opportunities and to voluntarily offer Leads at all levels of influence to access those Opportunities. The process is such a natural activity that they provide Leads during normal conversation without having to be asked. If viewing Allies in terms of a weighted percentage of ease of establishment to productivity, the Partner Ally would be the highest overall value. The Partner Ally is extremely tuned into identifying influential people, forming alliances, establishing a relationship, and logging them into both their mental and physical database. And the most important quality they possess is that they have the talent to match their best Allies with your specific need.

During a conversation, you can describe any aspect of your Target, be it the type of decision-maker, the territory, or the industry, and the Partner Ally will automatically scan their mental list of people and offer some form of introduction during normal conversation. I have been in meetings over coffee, or simply touched base through email, when the purpose was merely to catch up with a Partner Ally. After short exchanges of information, as in "What's new," I've been offered multiple, new key people whose organizations were potential customers or potential new Partner Allies.

In a LinkedIn email I received from a Partner Ally, whom I hadn't communicated with in two years, she asked what I was doing. I told her, and by reflex, she offered to me a person as a potential Partner Ally who was selling a complementary product. This person called on the same type of decision-maker that I called on. We met, reviewed our needs, and he immediately offered to me a customer that he was about to close. I called the customer, met with them, and got creative to incentivize further business development with the new Partner Ally. I offered a credit to the customer for purchasing my product that could be used only to purchase my new Partner Ally's product. I closed the sale in two weeks. The sale was completed in one-twelfth the sales cycle with a Lead I had absolutely no interaction with prior to the initial communication.

How to Find Them

As in the search method used for finding potential Allies in general, for this specific Partner Ally category, the steps are both intuitive and analytical. Your intuition will be focused on the Contacts who you strongly believe possess this instinctual Mindset, as described earlier. If intuition isn't working, the alternative identification technique is to utilize the Categorization Equation, provided you've interacted with the potential Allies enough times to generate sufficient data.

The search process will incorporate various databases, including electronic lists, business card inventories, social media associates, and your own memory. These lists should be viewed with the focused objective of deciding whether they possess the characteristic Mindset of this category.

Lastly, it will be necessary to populate the lists with new potential Allies, as this is the first principle of the Allies process—hunting for people. Prospecting for new Partner Allies follows a seven-step process and is productive by nature because it's forming alliances between individuals who will inherently possess mutually beneficial Mindset characteristics.

The Partner Ally 7-Step Prospecting Method

Step 1: Identify a complementary industry. Determine what industries sell to the same type of decision-maker or are a potential vertical industry for your product.

Step 2: Identify a complementary organization in that industry. Identify an organization with selling needs that are complementary to your own. (This is not the same as pursuing an individual organization to sell.)

Step 3: Identify a person in the organization who can create a mutually beneficial relationship. This can be any person at any level.

Step 4: Organize the names. Keep a list: Excel, Covve, black book, napkins, whatever is your preference.

Step 5: Communicate and meet. An initial meeting of any kind is required to discuss business development, and once you meet with the Lead, they become a Contact.

Step 6: Exchange general information and Target information. Several key characteristics must be determined initially before searching for the right people. The basic parameters which determine the perfect Target customer are:

1. Industry
2. Company Size
3. Geographic Territory
4. Decision-Maker

Other specific parameters are often needed to further isolate matching customers and will emerge during the review. But, in the simplest form, you're identifying the parameters of your Ally's ultimate customer type and providing the parameters of yours. Below is an example of one of the original Parameter Questionnaires I've used:

Organization_____   Date_____

Industry/SIC Code_____

Annual Sales Volume

Up to 2 Million   _____

2 to10 Million   _____

10 to 25 Million   _____

25 to 50 Million   _____

50 to 100 Million   _____

100 to 500 Million   _____

500+ Million   _____

Employee Size

1-3   _____
4-9   _____
10-24   _____
25-49   _____
50-99   _____
100-249   _____
250-499   _____
500-999   _____
1000-2499   _____
2500-4999   _____
5000-14999   _____
15000-19999 _____
20,000+   _____

Best Contact Position/Level _____

Territory (if applicable)

Zip Code   _____

County   _____

State   _____

Databases

The advent of software-based databases has greatly increased the speed of this process. Once the parameters have been established, isolating the matching customer types is as easy as inputting the data into a CRM database and creating the list. Most modern software-database tools have some type of search tool based on basic filtering characteristics. Further isolation will require more manual analysis unless the software tools are more relevantly advanced.

Existing Customer Database

In most cases, you will have an existing customer base to access unless the sales position or the territory is brand new. Isolating the potential customers is relatively easy. The unorthodox selling associated with Tactical Prospecting now comes into play. You will be introducing the Partner Ally's product to your existing customers, and the Partner Ally will be introducing your product to theirs. If 90 percent of the sale is prospecting and 10 percent is negotiation, this is the negotiation part. If the Lead is your existing customer, in the Partner Ally's mind, they're already in the door. And this creates an Anchor Seeding-Counterweighing Scenario.

Anchor Seeding–Counterweighing

Anchor Seeding is the process of offering Leads to an Ally first before the Ally provides Leads to you. They can be introduced to the Ally or you can introduce their product to the Lead yourself. The Leads will match the Ally's Target characteristics. This accomplishes two things. First, it will provide a baseline that the Ally will either meet or surpass by providing Leads in return. Second, it will determine the Ally's value by the level or the existence of Lead reciprocity. It is a monitoring tool that provides feedback as to whether they offer, in return, more Leads, an equal number of Leads, or no Leads at all.

Counterweighing determines the level of reciprocity and provides the index value for categorization of the Ally. I want to expand on this concept because it's a bit radical in its behavior but powerful when employed.

I was stuck in my thinking as to why this process worked so well. Although the results were evident, I couldn't figure out why I was gaining more appointments with my own prospect Contacts when introducing my Allies' products to them, than I was gaining by cold calling strangers to introduce my own product. Intuitively, I thought that since I knew my product and could pitch it better than my Ally's product, I should gain more appointments cold calling for myself. But the opposite was true. And then it came to me. The difference is based on the whole premise of Tactical Prospecting: familiarity breeds comfort. With an almost comical realization, I discovered that it was easier to get an appointment promoting *another* company's product to people I knew than it was pitching *my own* product to people I didn't know. That's when I reached the conclusion that will make every sales trainer cringe: much of the sale is made during the prospecting. It isn't made with product training, "closing the holes in the rabbit fence," reciting the feature, advantage, benefits of a Frisbee, or any recycled techniques taught once you're in the door. It's all in the setup; the rest is just negotiation.

Prospect Databases

Customer Relationship Management Database tools, CRMs are in virtually every organization and are required by Management to continually be monitored, accessed, and updated. The data consists of both existing customers and new prospects in a market. Now, of course, the database is still only as

> **Customer Relationship Management Database (CRM):** a CRM is a software tool that provides a central location where organizations can store customer and prospect data, track interactions, and share this information throughout the organization.

valuable as the data entered; however, when the database is accurate and detailed, it is an invaluable tool for Tactical Prospecting. What will negatively affect the value is the time required to enter the information.

The productivity potential is the accessibility of prospects' basic parameters, but more importantly the true value is the availability of specific and timely notes—the "inside information" available to a Partner Ally that would have taken a great deal of time to uncover on their own. Information such as budgets, competitive vendors, tenure of decision-makers, and on, and on. Imagine if a Sale Professional could cold call an organization already knowing that it is the perfect matching-customer type, with the budget available to purchase, the decision-makers' status, the existing vendor, and whether they're a satisfied customer. Imagine knowing all that when walking in the door. If that were the case, then that wouldn't be cold calling, would it? Now imagine that your Partner Ally also provides an introduction; then it would be unthinkable to cold call ever again, even if you wanted to.

Personal Database

The personal database really consists of two old forms of record-keeping: a business card portfolio and a brain. The Mindset or ability to tactically prospect is such a natural behavior to a Partner Ally that they engage in the process through instinct. A Partner Ally's memory is certainly the quickest, if not best, source of relevant people. It's as if their neurons are wired to connect people with Opportunities. Once the working parameters of the matching customer are established, the spigot will open, and their personal database will come pouring out. Countless times I was given close to a dozen key people to communicate with in the first thirty minutes of these meetings before either one of us ever booted up our computers. As for the business cards, they will be readily available at the meeting and then handed to you with brief descriptions of the key individuals and the best way to communicate with them. In a perfect world—perfect meaning we both had all the time in the world, not having to rush back to our cubicles—we could instead call or visit these Leads immediately.

Step 7: Anchor Seed-Counterweigh

The interactions with Allies are a continuous two-way relationship. The Anchor Seeding mechanism provides an initial energizing stimulus to activate the process by offering Leads *to* the Partner Allies first, and whenever possible. You provide what they need first and never wait for them. The Lead is the seeding activity that acts both as a stimulus, engaging the process with a new Ally, and as a monitor to assess their desire and ability to provide productivity in return. In the Alliance-building process, it is the device used to determine which potential Allies can be depended on and to Counterweigh the seeding in the form of a return Lead. This is the best way to determine if they are worth your time moving forward.

After the initial discussions are concluded and all the information is gathered, you will have a portrait of the ideal customer type for your Partner Ally. It is crucial to Anchor Seed. The more help you can provide immediately, the better. The reason for this isn't necessarily because of goodwill or to offer charity to receive charity in return—it's nothing of the kind. It is pure and simple to determine as quickly as possible if the new Partner Ally belongs in that category by expressing the proper Mindset. Anchor Seeding provides a snapshot of the behavior of the new Ally. If they respond to the action with immediate action—by following up with the prospect—that's the first step. Immediate action means immediate meetings, escorting the Partner Ally directly into the prospect's office, or initiating the first step with one of the suggested marketing methods previously discussed. Unless there has been some type of positive action experienced by the Partner Ally, the relationship will die on the vine and all the previous time will be wasted. The more-important next step is if they respond in kind.

Partner Ally Mechanisms

Due to the powerful Mindset of a Partner Ally, many types of mechanisms can be employed to generate a multitude and variety of qualified Leads. There is no limit to the creative ways in which these mechanisms can be built and instituted because the Partner Ally will always be open to new forms of business development and understand the intention of each tactic. Some mechanisms will address general Leads, while others will be designed to isolate specific Targets, regions, or verticals. It is like discovering the oil fields and building various machines to extract the oil.

The Lead-Exchange Mechanism

A standard method used to identify and exchange prospects with a Partner Ally is the Lead Exchange. This mechanism formalizes a process that provides efficiency with identification and efficiency with speed. By isolating specific characteristics of a matching customer, speed is gained in the sales process in the form of valuable information about the decision-makers, the organization, and even the "pain points." This information can be accessed by exchanging notes about organizations derived through personal interactions and the information entered in the CRM database. Although the Partner Ally will provide their Contacts according to many of these parameters, the information gained with a Lead-Exchange mechanism provides much greater detail.

The basic necessary parameters are:

1. Organization
2. Industry
3. SIC Code
4. Annual Sales Volume
5. Employee Size
6. Key Person
7. Key Person Position/Level
8. Territory
9. Zip Code
10. County
11. State
12. News/Latest Updates on Prospect

Below is an example questionnaire I've used:

```
                    PROSPECT SUMMARY ANALYSIS


Entity Name:

Contact Information:

Product/Service:

SIC Code:

Management:

Connection:

Decision Maker:

Connection:

Entity Contact:

Connection:

Connections:

SIC Connection:

Existing SIC Connection:

News:
```

Tactical Prospecting Mechanism

At the point when the Allies have established a trustworthy production level, you can institute advanced-networking techniques. These methods are more detailed and take a collaborative effort between the administrative departments of the Allies' respective organizations—for instance, the marketing department or finance department. I say this as a precaution, because before any of these marketing efforts are addressed, it is important to determine the relationship strength of the Ally to determine if that degree of effort is worth the time. And I'll warn you that although the Partner Ally will have a Mindset, the people in these departments that are engaged probably don't. So, as brilliant as the plan may be, it usually requires a lot of convincing.

Share-the-Cost Mechanism

When Partner Allies are profiting by satisfying the overlapping needs of each other's customers, then cooperative deals can be structured where all participating Allies can share the cost of the products sold. Through a myriad of mathematical, manufacturer, or miscellaneous credits originating from one Partner Ally's company offered to another Partner Ally's product, the net cost to the customer can be reduced. The products will, of course, complement each other in both application and need. This provides an incentive for the customers to purchase only from the Partner Allies involved and creates a type of prospecting loyalty program.

To replace misplaced loyalty, a brilliant marketing technique was offered by an internet service provider. They would use a portion of the overall value of the service they sold and offer that dollar amount as a credit to a vendor selling a needed complementary product. In this case, a customer was in the market for phone and internet service. The internet service provider offered that service, and a hardware vendor offered the needed hardware for the service. In this example, the hardware vendor was trying to sell a customer their product and quoted the price at $100,000. They would then introduce the internet service provider to the deal, and they quoted a price for their service for the entire contract term of $500,000. The internet service provider was willing to use 10 percent, or $50,000, of the quoted service and offer it as a credit toward hardware cost, which effectively reduced that cost by $50,000, cutting it in half. Of course, when a hardware vendor could beat their competitors' bids by 50 percent with no loss in profit, all their present and future customers were sent directly to their Partner Ally working at the internet service provider.

And another example of a Sales Professional employing Tactical Prospecting methods without knowing it: *The supervisors of the internet service provider directed all that business to a favored Sales Professional. He attributed his success to cold calling and "miraculously" made President's Club every year, not to mention three times the compensation of the actual cold-calling Sales Professionals. (Okay, I vented.) Again, I'm not complaining about that relationship; I am exposing the meaningless repudiation of other prospecting methods. My methods are the same by a different name. And if allowed, they would have gained for me those same President's Club trips.*

As I said earlier, this favoritism between supervisors and Sales Professional is a Process Ally that was then recategorized into a Partner Ally. And I would have been wasting my valuable time trying to change it, instead of participating in it. However, in this case, I could do neither.

The Mini-Expo Mechanism

Creating an exposition with a theme is a Tactical Prospecting mechanism that can yield multiple Opportunities if, as repeatedly stated, it is structured properly. The premise is that familiarity breeds comfort as it also breeds, in this case, a free lunch. A facility is chosen to stage the event.

I have formed these "mini-expos," utilizing three types of participants and a specific theme. Employing three organizations and accessing their customer and prospect databases, a marketing communication is created to advertise the event, a postcard, email flyer, brochure, or all three. A brochure proves very useful because it can also be used as a handout to potential participants at the event. The marketing piece is distributed to each of the three organizations' database of prospects approximately four to six weeks prior to the event. Then if the resources are available, follow-up communications are made about a week before. Now, the plan is that the three participant organizations have complementary products and customer types; therefore, each of the participant organizations will sell their product to one or all the other two organizations prospect attendees. It's best structured when there are two similarly sized organizations and a third, large, well-known organization as an anchor. The anchor organization's main product would be the most directly connected to the theme, to improve the response rate of potential attendees. For instance, an internet-service provider could be the anchor and an internet-based security service, and a security camera vendor could be the smaller organization presenters. Presentations are given by representatives of each organization with an important Q&A session after each. The presenter should be in sales at some level, if possible because the Q&A are specific to the individual prospects' situation. The interaction is designed to gain a follow-up appointment, and in many cases, this happens immediately after the event.

The Mini-Expo typically yields a 0.5 percent attendance rate, so in this case, five thousand prospect businesses were solicited and twenty-five attended. Hold on, your impulse may be telling you that's a worse success rate than cold calling. Not so. Remember, you're not knocking on five thousand doors and expending that unthinkable quantity of time. There would be a mass communication tool contacting five thousand potential or existing customers already in the database, not cold. To knock on five thousand doors would take how long—weeks, months? And to do it to an isolated specific vertical would take even longer. Also, the quality and superior closing ratio of a prospect voluntarily coming to an event, aware of its purpose and familiar with the vendors, wouldn't be in the same universe as a cold-called prospect. I don't want to waste your time calculating the enormous length of time it would take to knock on five thousand doors. Simply compare it with prospecting five thousand businesses for a one-day Mini-Expo.

The Resource-Sharing Mechanism

The most radical of the partnering mechanisms are available after building a trusted, long-term relationship with the Partner Ally. There have been times when one organization doesn't quite have the resources of another; however, does have the access to prospects due to tenure in a market or their individual tenure in an industry. In either case, Resource Sharing can be employed to prospect for a partner's complementary product when a need is identified, thereby helping gain an appointment. Resources such as your own marketing department or in-house telemarketers can be used to contact prospects for the other Partner Ally's organization. An appointment can then be gained for both parties with a single matching decision-maker.

The Formal Tactical Partnership Mechanism

A Formal Tactical Partnership can be formed through a contractual obligation between organizations. This tends to be more complicated and often this requires a meeting of the minds between departments in different organizations. Incorporating one company's service offering into another's product line and rebranding the service is an example of this. Individual contractual requirements of each department unfortunately can also spell out extensive details and time. Therefore, it's important to be extremely cognizant of the ratio of time to results, in order to determine whether the expended effort required with this type of partnership will be worth the expected production. Some of the potential pitfalls will be incorporating into the process other departments and their personnel who don't have the Mindset, and subsequently don't comprehend the necessity of the process or their role. Hence, they overcomplicate the process and create their own version of prospecting obstacles. What is most important with any Tactical Prospecting method is that it must be worked properly after establishing the partnership for it to succeed. What is clear, but often forgotten, is that these prospecting mechanisms don't run on autopilot.

The Final Ally Categories

Before I continue with the last two categories—POS Ally and Party Ally—I want to make clear that they should be viewed as categories distinct from the first three, rather than as one that follows them in any sort of logical progression. However, formatting the categories in this manner makes it systematic and shows how the categories relate to each other. The difference is that they require much more time and structure to establish; however, the payoff is enormous.

CHAPTER 8

The Party Ally

"A Think Tank for Leads"

THE PARTY ALLY IS an agreed-upon relationship established with people who gather in a single location for business-development brainstorming. These high-value Allies are a think tank for identifying Leads and creating Contacts. The dynamic is so extensive that I'm concerned about the description limiting the comprehension of its power. When multiple Allies with a Business-Development Mindset are in the same collaborative environment, it forms a synergy for the identification of powerful Leads that couldn't be accomplished by communicating with them individually.

The Components of a Party Ally

1. Party Ally Participants

A minimum of three participants is required. There probably is a maximum number, however, in my experience, I haven't reached a number of participants great enough that it affected the productivity of the meeting. The participants should be from related but distinct industries, while the Targets should remain complementary. This structure promotes open communication between participants and multiple participants promotes a belief and validity of the process.

The Lead production generated from the Party Ally is due to two rationales: First, there is a higher likelihood that the participants have valuable knowledge because they've most likely had some type of communication with Targets. This is directly through their own communication or indirectly through a network of their own Allies. Either way, there is always a huge overlap of information when the Targets are complementary. Second, there is no privacy issue if there are representative participants from different industries. There's less a fear of speaking openly if the participants are not concerned that their database of key influential people will be stolen since no real competitors are in the room.

2. Moderator

Since there is a tendency for the meeting to become extremely active and possibly disorganized, it works best when a moderator is present. A moderator can be both a participant and something of an information referee, not because the participants need to be contained due to disruptive behavior, but merely because some communication exchanges can become voluminous, and items can be missed. Also, the moderator acts as a transcriber, keeping notes on the information being discussed. There is a third responsibility that can be managed only by individuals with advanced understanding of the process. While the discussions are active, the moderator can search many of the available databases, analyzing the key influential people that are being offered at that moment, and attempting to expand on an Ally's network. Finally, they can also access these databases to kickstart the process if it starts too slowly or stalls; however, this rarely happens.

As I mentioned earlier, once established, a Process Ally may fit into any other category, depending on their Business-Development Mindset. One of the best examples of "recategorized" Allies is an existing sales team. Sales Professionals working for an organization typically possess all the features of a Party Ally: tenure, industry knowledge, powerful Business-Development Mindset, and complementary Targets. This provides an immediate source of productive Allies already on the payroll regularly contained within a Lead-producing workshop called the sales meeting.

The Party Ally Process

The participants should have some type of access to their database of people, whether it is a laptop to view a CRM and websites, or as simple as a business card binder filled with names of their colleagues. This is, of course, in addition to the best prospecting database tool there is: their brain. Although any type of Target can be the focus of the meeting, a product will be the most beneficial to the participants. Any Leads offered that could benefit from a specific product will be further along the prospecting process, closer to making a sale.

The review of the product will include a basic description of features and, most importantly, the key-value differentiators. Next, the ideal matching industry, matching customer, and matching decision-makers are described and highlighted. As the discussion commences and the identities of potential Leads are communicated, the moderator records the information, accesses database information, and, if necessary, maintains control of the flow. The participants are engaging in the same information gathering as the moderator; however, the difference is that the moderator should refrain from communicating proactively with the Leads that they're researching. Their responsibility is to maintain the flow of information.

Party Ally Mechanisms

Open-Source Party Ally

The Open-Source Party Ally is a "free for all" for disseminating Leads associated with a variety of Targets. There are no specific boundaries limiting the discussion to specific product features, customer types, or Lead characteristics. The tactic is to gain Leads by both matching prospects directly and indirectly, related to the ultimate sale of each Ally's product. Since the participants have a very strong Mindset, a discussion of each product and its main benefits will stimulate other beneficial aspects and conjure other types of potential customers, possibly not thought of previously. Although organizations can also be spotlighted, the product should be the focus of interaction. The participants don't have to necessarily have a direct relation to the product. Each participant can have their own objectives in mind; however, the product focus is used to provide a theme to inspire the discussion and direction of the communications.

In addition to all categories of Allies, brand-new Contacts or Leads can also participate to ideally create a minimum of three Party Allies once the interaction takes place. This ensures that the session will be productive if it turns out that one or all the new participants have a weak Mindset or worse, are in self-destruct mode due to any personal issue under the sun.

I arranged a meeting with two Passive Allies. When the three of us met, it appeared that one of them had lost motivation to participate and behaved unprofessionally on many levels. The event was doomed from the start.

Product Party Ally

The Product Party Ally objective is to isolate matching prospects for one specific product. The Ally participants should optimally be from complementary industries, as this will provide a larger number of related backgrounds of the Leads in their personal and customer databases. Also, through the synergy created from overlapping industries, there will be an increased flow of information. A bevy of Leads and general best practices will emerge to facilitate the creation of new Targets.

Sales Meeting Party Ally

The ideal Party Ally event is an organization's sales meeting, since they are already mandatory participants and are being paid for by the organization. The tremendous amount of knowledge overlap of Sales Professionals from the same organization can produce a greater number of qualified Leads than all the typical prospecting techniques combined. In addition to the personal database of a Sales Professional, there is also specific knowledge on vertical industries due to their specialties and relationships formed by the most tenured along their career path. I'm labeling the sales meeting as a Party Ally event even though it does consist of a salesforce initially gathered to discuss other sales topics. The difference with a Party Ally event operating in this environment is the agenda will be one of Tactical Prospecting, not the typical itinerary of a sales meeting. It has the objective of obtaining the identities of Leads specific to a single Sales Professional's needs.

In the hundreds of sales meetings, I've participated in, it always amazed me how much untapped information could be extracted from professionals with the supposed Mindset for prospecting compared with any other profession. With the typical, regularly occurring sales meetings, the discussion was usually the sales forecast, the problems with paperwork, and the job threats if neither improved. What if, instead, the Party Ally Process was instituted regularly, with five or eight or thirty Sales Professionals in the same room, bringing with them an average tenure of ten years? This mechanism could potentially offer fifty or eighty or three hundred years' worth of Contacts to exchange. If one-on-one meetings with Partner Allies can generate a dozen possible qualified appointments in two hours, imagine the appointment ratio of thirty Sales Professionals. As I said in the beginning, the productivity is exponential.

You may be asking, if a Sales Professional possesses a list of their own Contacts, why wouldn't they be apprehensive about making it public? Well, first, if they don't understand Tactical Prospecting, then they quite possibly don't know how to properly develop such a list or have one that's easily accessible. Often, they don't realize the power of these relationships they've developed in the first place. Second, if they do have one, they'll be motivated to participate openly if they also are receiving Contacts from the other participants. And since there is a team, in the "physically together" sense, not the collaboration cliché sense, the informality will make the process comfortable and even productively enjoyable. When was the last time you heard the term *enjoyable* used to describe a prospecting method? Their business development juices will start flowing as they become willing participants.

The only potential pitfall is if the process is used to manipulate one willing participant for the benefit of another. Then the event becomes a figurative Anchor Seeding with the victim being saddled with a figurative anchor. A simple warning signal for this or any other pitfall encountered with any Alliance Process is if when providing Leads, a colleague's only response is:

"Keep 'em comin'."

Don't!

To avoid this scenario, Management must ascertain the characteristics of the participants and make the proper adjustments ahead of time. This can be accomplished by setting the objectives of the meeting and giving the participants a "heads up" as to the agenda and the expectations. However, the "warning" strategy will need to be only a temporary fix. The real long-term solution will be to hire Sales Professionals with the Mindset in the first place.

Initiating the process can be as simple as a Sales Professional stating openly, "I am trying to get into account XYZ," and the associated Contacts immediately stream out from colleagues. And if no Contacts are immediately forthcoming, then the interaction of the moderator and prospecting tools aid that process. Any Leads that are discovered through these tools may not be as directly connected to the participants' Allies as you'd like. But often, indirect connections to Leads appear with these tools and can provide just as much value. You should be starting to see how the Alliance process can generate such a high appointment rate, certainly in comparison to the bombardment of Management's vacant sales meetings.

I was used to fill a vacancy when I arrived at a regularly scheduled eight a.m. sales meeting, which for me required a two-hour commute. The sales VP walked in, said, "Good morning," and proclaimed, "Well, I don't really have anything for you today."

I thought, Nothing? Really! You mean on the way into the office, you couldn't think of a single sales topic to discuss with your salesforce? I often pointed out to Management that certain issues or entire meetings would be more economically productive if held with a conferencing tool. But in this case, even that wouldn't have been true, because nothing can be produced when there's nothing to say.

The positive bend on this episode was that he didn't create some fake topic just to make the meeting seem valuable. He immediately exposed his vacant agenda, and we cut our losses. Do you think he would've had something to say if he was operating on his own dime, commission-wise? How many other sales meetings expended the same amount of time to simply recite a forecast we'd never achieve or to update an administrative procedure that didn't benefit sales in the first place.

Just once, when asked for a sales forecast, I'd like to answer that question with, "I'm going to sell four less hours of quota than I would've if I didn't have to drive here to tell you that." However, this point was finally accepted, and the future sales meetings were conducted on a video-conferencing tool. They were now in more relaxed environments with a more efficient use of time. As a result, sales strategy discussions began with little prompting and a continual exchange of business contacts between the participants.

Internet-Based Party Ally

Although the Party Ally Process can be a complicated undertaking unless it's a scheduled gathering like a sales meeting, there are many web-based interfaces that can make the process certainly easier and, in some ways, quicker than typical face-to-face meetings. They're commonplace and extraordinary for creating reach, as they can more easily access the number of participants, the availability of participants, and the breadth of participants. By merely sending an invite and a link, a literal global Party Ally event can be gathered immediately in one place. All that remains is communicating the intent of the meeting and the theme.

CHAPTER 9

The POS Ally

"The Channel Partner"

A POINT-OF-SALE (POS) Ally is an agreed-upon relationship established with a person who controls a business that's structured to resell your product. Without a doubt, the POS Ally provides the highest production value to a Sales Professional. The complete sales process from product introduction to customer identification and the final closing of the sale is performed by the POS Ally with minimal investment of your time. It may not appear to be a typical Ally as described in the preceding categories; however, gaining access to other people's "entities of productivity" and converting them into other Allies is the main success criteria of the Alliance process. "Entities of productivity," or Targets, can come in the form of information, people, or other organizations. In this case, the POS Ally assumes the selling function for your own business in exchange for some agreed-upon form of compensation. The productivity value is a result of new people and new organizations being converted into both closed sales and new Allies in the time it takes to establish the partnering relationship with the POS Ally. To successfully create a POS Ally, three objectives must be fulfilled:

1. Your product must be special.

The offering in some way must be unique, so it creates a differentiator for the POS Ally and provides them an advantage over their competition. The unique characteristics can be aspects of the product or aspects of your organization in terms of how you conduct business with POS Allies.

2. Your product and your organization must be reliable.

The trustworthy nature of the organization is paramount; otherwise, the other two objectives will be meaningless. A POS Ally's new and existing customers are their lifeblood, and these customers will attribute all things directly to them. Any negative behavior generated from your organization is, in the customer's view, the POS Ally's negative behavior. There is no separation. Whatever emanates through the POS Ally, regardless of the origin, is theirs to own. Their customers do not make any distinction. Therefore, the POS Ally is overly sensitive to the risk of damaging that relationship.

3. The compensation must be worth it.

The compensation must be great enough to justify diverting their valuable time to selling your products. The POS Ally is either reselling an existing product through another competitive organization or is researching the possibility of selling yours. In either case, there will be many characteristics of your competition that need to be equaled or surpassed by your complete offering. One of those key characteristics is the amount of monetary compensation that can be made reselling your product, especially if you're trying to knock out the incumbent.

The Two Types of POS Allies

There are two types of POS Allies: POS Partner and a POS Reseller. Each can be formed in virtually any situation. However, depending on the industry there are models that create a better fit for one or the other. The differences are found in the method in which they conduct business in relation to their industries. A POS Partner contains all the characteristics of a POS Reseller, including owning an established base of customers, actively pursuing new customers, and marketing the same basic product being sold by the Sales Professional. The only difference is that a POS Partner provides products and services that complement the product you're selling and offer Targets as compensation in return. These Targets can be anything of value, from information to the ultimate sale to a customer.

A POS Reseller has an existing customer base, unless it's a new business, and they actively pursue new customers. They are supplied with and sell the Sales Professional's product as their main product and are solely structured, designed, and compensated for reselling the Sales Professional's product. The product cost structure, pricing, marketing, and selling functions all consider the method of resale distribution in their design.

The POS Partner also has an existing customer base and actively pursues new customers; however, their business model is built on a different main product that is associated only in some way with the Sales Professional's product. It will complement the POS Partner's main product as a value add-on, a dissimilar product with similar benefits, or a completely separate product that can satisfy the needs of the same customer type. POS Partners prefer Leads or a monetary fee, usually a one-time commission as compensation for the resale of your product.

In either case, the key factor in establishing a POS Ally relationship from a POS Contact is the structure of the deal. As these entities are active self-sustaining businesses, the level of compensation and ease of creating a relationship are the most important determining factors to these decision-makers.

POS Partner Ally

A POS Partner Ally is one that is not typical for the specific industry. It is similar to a regular Partner Ally, with the Lead-producing potential of a Party Ally. This is because they possess the proper Mindset for Tactical Prospecting and a customer base that matches your product, even if they don't presently market your product. Once a POS Partner Ally is identified, all that remains is properly structuring a mutually beneficial deal in which they get the proper compensation, and you get access to the proper Targets.

A POS Partner Ally is like a Partner Ally that is a business entity. It possesses all the advantages of an operating business, including a customer base, new customer acquisition, and operational structure to assist with marketing the products. Now as I mentioned earlier, compensation paid to them can mean financial compensation or payment in the form of customer Leads. There is a definite compensation preference depending on the type of POS Ally and the structure of a specific industry. Some industries are well-suited and have a distribution model specifically set up to resell a product and receive some type of monetary payment. However, with the POS Partner Ally, the type of distribution is not a typical model for the industry and, as such, isn't financially designed to offer a percentage of a sale. This isn't an obstacle, because in this case, the POS Partner would prefer customer Leads as payment, which have a vastly greater value to them. If the volume of sales increases to a level where the monetary payment becomes more attractive, then the compensation structure could change. But in that case, they would become a POS Reseller, and you have possibly created a new distribution strategy for that industry.

The POS Partner will have a customer base and will be proactively growing their base of new customers. When researching the right type of POS Partner, it is crucial that there are some complementary characteristics between both of your products. In a non-traditional relationship such as this, the POS Partner Ally has little patience for a unique venture that does not show immediate potential. The initial sales pitch will have to succinctly describe the symbiotic relationship of the two products. Once this is explained, then there will be time to probe and learn more about their business, their goals, and their sales model. After you have learned these things, then structuring the compensation of the deal becomes much easier. You will be able to determine what type of compensation makes the most sense from the perspective of your business and, most importantly, the type of compensation most valuable to the Partner.

At the end of the meeting, you should both have all the necessary information to begin establishing Leads for each other. Just as there are end-user customers that require products with complementary functionality, there are POS Partners that can offer that complementary product to a customer as an additional value. The key similarities of the POS Allies are that they both market your product to their account base and provide a means of identifying new customers. The main productivity value is that their effort goes directly to a sale, with less need for forming intermediary Alliance-process components, such as making a Contact through a Significant Interaction, then establishing an agreed-upon relationship. The POS Allies create an Ally for you by creating the sale for them.

I formed a complementary partnership while developing a territory for an office equipment business. I built a relationship with a supplier that sold, among other things, pre-owned versions of our main product line. They didn't have a certified dealership with the major equipment manufacturer, so they could sell used equipment, but not new equipment. Although they were missing out on potential sales of new equipment, their main revenue stream was providing maintenance on the used equipment. So, right away I knew that the value to them would be offering the maintenance accounts of our customers who owned older equipment, and in exchange they would offer me the customers requiring new equipment. Although we may have been losing a maintenance account, to us they were not as cost effective as selling and maintaining new equipment. The relationship was a mutually beneficial, simple exchange and was easy to establish. I handed them old equipment accounts, which they needed, and they handed me new equipment sales, which we needed.

Steps to Establish a POS Partner Ally

Step 1: Identify businesses that call on the same type of decision-maker.

Step 2: Identify businesses that sell products and services complementary to your products and services.

Step 3: Communicate with the business's decision-maker and set up a meeting to discuss the process.

Step 4: Probe to find out the most valuable compensation structure for the Partner.

Step 5: Anchor Seed.

Step 6: Expect a Counterweight.

The Anchor-Seeding concept not only initiates the Lead process but also sets a standard value level depending on the value of productivity that's offered to the Partner. Presumably, the Counterweight will be of equal or greater value to the Sales Professional. Nevertheless, the intention of Anchor Seeding is for the Ally to communicate to you what's valuable to them, and you provide that valuable thing as quickly as possible.

POS Reseller Ally

The POS Reseller Ally not only is significantly more productive than the POS Partner Ally but also provides the most productivity of all the Allies available to a Sales Professional. They're a specialized form of sales distribution established for specific industries. The difference between a POS Partner and a POS Reseller is that with a Reseller the structure of that specific industry is properly suited for a resale channel and has specifically been established for this type of distributor. The business structure is specifically designed to resell the Sales Professional's product directly to new and existing end-user customers.

The power of a POS Reseller lies in their reach within a territory and familiarity with their customer base. The number of Resellers within a territory is not limited by the cost structure of your own organization. The only restrictions are those decided by the territorial market and what it can handle. The familiarity with their existing or potential customers can often provide a less competitive selling environment and a more rapid sales cycle. The sales volume is potentially exponential if compared with a physical sales force of "feet on the street." If individual Sales Professionals are viewed as points of distribution in one-to-one selling scenarios, then the sales revenue is limited to what can be gained in a set time period. Consequently, if the sales revenue is limited, then the costs of increasing these "points of distribution" are limiting as well. But if the number of POS Resellers is limited only by what the market can sustain, then a sales force of Resellers can provide the maximum amount of sales revenue in a market with costs merely associated with the percentage of revenue paid by your organization as commission.

Add into the equation an existing customer base owned by each Reseller and what remains is a much greater number of selling entities multiplied by the number of familiar customers to sell. Adding to this:

When I was the VP of sales for a telecommunications company, the product radically changed and, as a result, the Target customer also changed. For a long time, the target was a business customer and the average salesperson sold seventy units per month. Then, virtually overnight, the new target customer changed from a business to an individual consumer. The distribution model had to change to a Partner-Reseller model rather than individual Sales Professionals prospecting individual businesses. The product, the price, then the Reseller sales had such an immediate impact that the sales volume increased from thirty-five units per day for the salesforce to one thousand units per day. As the product characteristics and the reduced price point were key components needed to reach the consumer, the typical prospecting and sales methods used to sell businesses could in no way produce the same volume sold to individual consumers. As a result of the new ability to reach consumers, a different resale distribution model was created, and the sales volume skyrocketed.

And born from this new POS Reseller Ally were other significant positive structural changes in the business operation itself. Since most of the sales were generated through a network of Resellers, the Sales Professionals had to change their prospecting role. Their new responsibilities involved negotiating partnerships with these business entities and then managing them. With the tremendous addition of volume and Management requirements, their personal compensation also needed to change from commission-based to a pure salaried sales position. You may be thinking that a salaried Sales Professional would have little incentive to produce without a commission reward. But in fact, the opposite was true; they were tremendous producers because they could now concentrate in a manner that was intelligent and responsible, and they prioritized the best interest of the organization. There was no longer a commission structure that could be manipulated; they just did "good" business.

Another "good" was that the recruitment process for new Sales Professionals was rational and simplified. Although it was deliberate, it was not necessarily slow, because many applicants were recommendations from other qualified employees. The new hires proved to be highly motivated employees for many reasons, the strongest of which was the organization's ability to attract people with a Tactical Mentality. The continual addition of quality Sales Professionals created a competitive selling environment.

POS Reseller Compensation

The most attractive compensation structure for a POS Reseller is a commission paid on a recurring residual basis. Now, granted, this compensation structure is most attractive to most businesses, but a POS Reseller's business model and the owners themselves are inherently pre-conditioned to receive this type of commission. If a onetime commission payment—or worse, Leads are offered as compensation to a POS Reseller—the deal will be doomed from the start. As the proper Mindset is the key to the strength of the Tactical Prospecting Ally, the business Mindset of each type of Ally is just as important of a consideration. Remember, gaining

Allies employs selling techniques. When selling to a decision-maker, determining their Mindset and what they value is the result of the information-gathering process.

The best way to think about POS Resellers is as the business partners of your organization. They have established a business and have suffered all the stresses, risks, and financial obligations promoting your product to the public. You represent to them both a sales manager and business partner providing all the support they require because, literally, if they succeed, you succeed.

The POS Reseller may not appear to be a typical Ally; however, they, in fact, are the most productive of all. Remember that the main value of an Ally is to provide appointments on a continual basis. This is what's occurring even if the appointments are for themselves for their own business survival. The added difference and overriding value is that they also sell the appointment for you.

Finally, there are many types of POS Resellers. Some resell to the end-user, and some sell channel to channel. Their functions vary according to their product line, the end-user customer type, and their level within the channel. However, the basic requirements for interacting with the POS Ally are steadfast. You must provide them with something unique about the total offering as a differentiator, reliability of the product and organization, and the proper compensation. All three of these attributes are required to make it worth their effort to form a relationship.

The Tactical Result

There are a variety and abundance of positive process improvements gained by implementing necessary changes in a sales environment. As an unsolicited convenience, the sales environment will faithfully tell you when changes are necessary, if you're willing to listen. And the only reason these warnings are ignored by Management is that they're felt to be an inconvenience with little financial consequence. The sales environment is not only faithful but also generous, because when Management does pay attention to its needs and make the proper adjustments, it provides an unexpected bevy of positive consequences. In the previous example, by adopting the POS Reseller model, the organization received a multitude of serendipitous rewards which included:

- A thirty-fold increase in sales.
- A more compatible compensation plan that benefited the Sales Professionals and the organization.
- Greatly reduced administrative costs.
- An improved employee recruitment process and quality of hire.
- A virtually nonexistent sales employee turnover.
- A competitive advantage through the creation of an industry-pioneering distribution model.
- Greatly increased revenue by selling complementary products and reaching untapped markets.
- And many, many more.

By listening to what the sales environment was telling us, we created relationships with the most productive Ally, the POS Reseller. The positive unexpected changes impacted all aspects of the business because right in front of our eyes, we let sales do what it does best, fixes everything.

PART FOUR

Alliance Analytics

ALTHOUGH I'VE WORKED FOR a multitude of companies, I've interviewed in one form or another with many, many more. The discussions varied from typical pleasantries, general topics about their core business practices, or specifics about my background. After a time, I had found that the only consistency emanating from these meetings was that, by the end of each, there were more uncertainties than existed when I first walked in the door.

When I asked the interviewer how much money I could make, the question was never accurately answered. The irony was that when the question was answered, I ultimately earned more than their answer. And when the amount of money I could make was volunteered by the interviewer without me asking, I always earned less. The interviewers lacked a thorough understanding of the sales position and relied on anecdotal data to support their figures. They simply provided convenient information. And what was most convenient to them was reciting the typical prospecting mantras as the means to earning the amount of money they purported, such as "If you knock on one hundred doors a day" or "Make fifty calls an hour." I knew from my experience that these methods could in no way produce the sales revenue they professed. As I left each interview, the first unanswered question was always, "Realistically, how much can I make?"

As the interview discussion moved to describing the daily sales duties, the requirements usually consisted of a standard set of sales activities. This occurred even when I was interviewing as an independent consultant, presumably recruited because I possessed a unique set of sales-prospecting skills. In their mind, there was no conflict with the typical prospecting tasks and the specialized prospecting methods they knew I used. The second unanswered question was, "How much can I earn if forced to share prospecting time with other mandatory tasks?"

Finally, from the moment I agreed to an interview, I had a monetary figure in mind. This is a goal amount of money I wanted to earn, regardless of whether that goal was to pay monthly bills, buy a house, or to attain some level of wealth. I have found that it is more useful to determine the value of a new position by comparing it to a preset goal rather than whether it's simply more money than the previous position. The final question I asked, which remained unanswered, was, "How much do I have to earn to reach my goal?"

What I needed was the ability to use the data provided by the organization to calculate the answers to the following questions:

1. *How much will I earn?*

2. *How much am I being forced to earn?*

3. *How much do I have to earn?*

Alliance Analytics is the collection, recording, and unbiased analysis of sales-prospecting metrics. It is the second key principle of Tactical Prospecting. Measurement is the most essential activity involved in prospecting, as it acts as the key control element of your time. It provides the tactical feedback mechanism required to implement, adjust, or discard prospecting methods.

> **The Three Principles of Tactical Prospecting:**
> 1. The least-investment of time
> 2. *Measurement*
> 3. Identification of a Business-Development Mindset in others

The problem with the present sales environment is that metrics have become a negligent practice that has, at best, been degraded to a level of oblivion and, at worst, become a tool for propaganda. The metrics values produced by the Sales Professional are the most necessary, and yet the most lacking, pieces of information gathered by Management. They are lacking in availability, accuracy, and, most importantly, interpretation. The commonly proposed concept is that if a Sales Professional does something, then something will happen, and if they do that "something" more, then more of that thing will happen. This is indicative of the limitations of Management thinking. It's true as a stimulus-response activity, but completely useless as a tactical plan designed to generate specific results in a specific time period. Or, putting it simply, it is a completely useless tactic to generate real productivity. Too often, superficial productivity measurements are merely used by Management as numeric versions of bias designed to justify failing sales results, finger-pointing, or a poor work ethic. The quantifiable results of your efforts which are used to form successful prospecting activities must be identified and isolated. Otherwise, you'll be proverbially prospecting in the wind, and supervisors will always manage to stay upwind.

On one of those windy days, I worked at an organization where the sales production was stagnant, and we were faced with daily threats of termination. The attempted remedies consisted of hiring new supervisors with new means of punishment. They hired a sales manager who implemented his philosophy. When that didn't work, they hired a director of sales, implementing another philosophy. When that didn't work, they hired a VP of sales, who implemented his philosophy, which was the same as the first guy's. And finally, when that didn't work, they ultimately hired an executive VP of sales to really "shake things up." In our first sales meeting with the new executive VP, he walked into the room paused for a moment, stared sternly at the sales team, and, with no greeting, forcefully recited, "If you work an extra hour at the beginning of the day and an extra hour at the end of the day, you will gain two extra hours per day, which turns into forty extra hours per month. Those forty extra hours per month is an extra week for every month, which becomes three extra months for every year. After ten years, you would have worked two and a half years more than the competition." He then turned and exited the room. I leaned over to my friend and whispered, "Why'd they hire this guy—to multiply?"

Numerical data is the quantification of your effort. Its accurate collection is the quintessential monitoring tool to provide the information needed to decide to continue a task, alter a task, avoid a task, or discard a task. Measurement of the activity is more important than the activity itself because it will determine whether to employ the tactics before wasted effort provides that information for you.

The Alliance Analytics Equations

The Alliance Analytics Equations are the tools to measure your effort, both in anticipation and outcome of a task. These equations produce reality. *In some cases, the solution to an equation has been rounded to the nearest whole number for manipulative ease and practicality.* They will determine whether there is any value with the use of your time and the amount of value that is produced with your time. They will allow to answer the questions:

- How much will I earn?

- How much am I being forced to earn?

- How much do I have to earn?

CHAPTER 10

How Much Will I Earn?

Prospecting Production

The Monthly Prospecting Production Equation

THE MONTHLY PROSPECTING Production Equation is used to calculate the production level within a selling environment by utilizing twelve sales components. The elegance of this tool is that it can be implemented in an unfamiliar selling environment by using the existing data already generated by the organization. If you are beginning a new sales position and trying to determine the potential for achieving your personal selling goals, this can be accomplished by inputting the data provided by the organization. If they are incapable of providing the data, that also offers insight into their sales-management capabilities. The equation can also provide the success rates necessary by various methods of prospecting to achieve anticipated production levels.

> **The Monthly Prospecting Production Equation should answer the question: How much will I earn?**

The equation reads as follows:

Monthly Prospecting Production =

$$\underbrace{\dfrac{\left((TPH\text{-}NPH) - \left(NCSAppt * NCSApptH\right) * \left(\tfrac{AveV}{MSC}\right) - \left(ECSAppt * ECSApptH * \left(\tfrac{AveV}{MSC}\right)\right) \right)}{\underbrace{\left(HPAppt + NCSApptH + \left(NCSApptH * \tfrac{(AveV-1)}{MSC}\right)\right)}_{\text{Hourly Time to Gain an Appointment}}}}_{} * \underbrace{MSC}_{\substack{\text{Months to}\\\text{Close a Sale}}} * \underbrace{\left((ARS * NCCR) + (ARS * ECSAppt * ECCR) \right)}_{\substack{\text{Total Revenue}\\\text{per Closing Ratio}}} * \underbrace{\tfrac{(MSC+1)}{2}}_{\substack{\text{Sales}\\\text{Cycle Factor}}}$$

(Bracket label over numerator: Total Available Prospecting Hours per Month)

The Components in the Equation:

1. Total Available Prospecting Hours (TPH)

The TPH is the total number of hours in a set period of time in which prospecting can be performed. This figure represents the total hours in a month that will be dedicated to prospecting. In our example, 173 represents the total number of available hours in a month. This will provide a production index value as a starting point if every available hour were dedicated to prospecting.

> **Total Prospecting Hours (TPH):** 2,080 working hours per year divided by 12 months will equal 173 hours per month.

2. Non-Prospecting Hours (NPH)

The NPH is the total number of hours in a set period of time in which prospecting is not performed. This figure is used to identify the time expended on activities other than prospecting. This helps identify your time distribution and whether these hours are assigned to productive or necessary activities.

3. New Customer Set Appointment Hours (NCSApptH)

The NCSApptH is the hourly time it takes to complete a new scheduled customer appointment. A new customer refers to a customer who is not producing revenue as part of the existing base of customers. These appointments characteristically take longer than appointments with existing customers and, as such, the appointment time should be isolated.

4. Average Customer Visits to Completion (AveV)

The AveV is the average number of visits to a prospect required to either complete a sale or end the engagement with no sale.

5. New Customer Set Appointments (NCSAppt)

The NCSAppt is the number of appointments with new customers that have been set at the beginning of the set time period being analyzed. If, at the beginning of a month, there are set appointments with new customers, those visits would take time away from prospecting time.

6. Existing Customer Set Appointment (ECSAppt)

The ECSAppt is the number of appointments with existing customers that have been set at the beginning of the set time period being analyzed. If, at the beginning of a month, there are set appointments with existing customers, those visits would take time away from prospecting time.

7. Existing Customer Set Appointment Hours (ECSApptH)

The ECSApptH is the average hourly time required to complete an existing customer-scheduled appointment.

8. Hourly Prospecting per Appointment (HPAppt)

The HPAppt is the average hourly prospecting time required to gain a new customer appointment using a specific prospecting method. This metric isolates the productivity level as time and compares various prospecting methods.

9. New Customer Closing Ratio (NCCR)

The NCCR is the closing sale ratio of a new customer appointment using a specific prospecting method. The characteristics of both a new customer and the prospecting method used to gain the appointment affect the closing ratio.

10. Existing Customer Closing Ratio (ECCR)

The ECCR is the closing-sale ratio of an existing-customer appointment. The characteristics of both an existing customer and the reason for the appointment affect the closing ratio and differ from the characteristics of a new prospect.

11. Average Revenue per Sale (ARS)

The ARS is the average revenue per sale. The revenue of a sale from both new and existing prospects are averaged.

12. Monthly Sales Cycle (MSC)

The MSC is the length of the sales cycle period in months. The monthly time from first communication to the close of the sale for both new and existing customers are averaged to determine the monthly sales cycle.

Real-World Sales Data

Let's analyze the data from a real-world example. What is interesting, but not surprising, was that these following metrics were provided by an organization and, as you'll see, didn't produce enough to satisfy even their own company sales goals. Regardless, the prospecting methods were still forced upon the sales team. I later found out that the prospecting methods weren't discarded, the salespeople were.

Data Examples:

Total Available Prospecting Hours	TPH	173
Non-Prospecting Hours	NPH	53
New Customer Set Appointment Hours	NCSApptH	2
Average Customer Visits to Completion	AveV	4
New Customer Set Appointments	NCSAppt	0
Existing Customer Set Appointments	ECSAppt	1
Existing Customer Appointment Hours	ECSApptH	2
Hourly Prospecting Time to Gain a New Customer Appointment	HPAppt	8
New Customer Appointment Closing Rate	NCCR	10%
Existing Customer Appointment Closing Rate	ECCR	15%
Average Revenue per Sale	ARS	$10,000
Monthly Sales Cycle	MSC	6

With the variables entered, the equation reads:

Monthly Prospecting Production =

$$\frac{\left(\left(\overbrace{(173\text{-}53)\text{-}(0^*2)}\ *\ \left(\frac{4}{6}\right)\text{-}\left(1^*2^*\left(\frac{4}{6}\right)\right)\right)\right)}{\underbrace{\left(\left(8+2+\left(2^*\frac{(4\text{-}1)}{6}\right)\right)\right)}}\ *\ \overbrace{\left((10{,}000^*10\%)+(10{,}000^*1^*15\%)\right)}\ *\ \overbrace{\frac{(6+1)}{2}}$$

Total Available Prospecting Hours per Month

Total Revenue per Closing Ratio

Sales Cycle Factor

Total Hours to Gain One Appointment

Months to Close a Sale (6)

Which becomes:

$$= \frac{\overbrace{10.79}^{\substack{\text{Total}\\\text{Appointments}}} * (\overbrace{\$2500}^{\substack{\text{Total Revenue}\\\text{per Closing Ratio}}} * \overbrace{3.5}^{\substack{\text{Sales Cycle}\\\text{Factor}}})}{\underbrace{6}_{\text{Months to Close a Sale}}}$$

Which becomes:

Average Sales Revenue per Month = $ 15,735

The Prospecting Productivity amount revealed that, according to the metrics provided by the supervisors, an average of $15,735 per month is what can be produced. This was determined before the Sales Professional had to knock on a single door. The example shows that by incorporating the available prospecting time, the production metric from the existing prospecting method, the average revenue amount per sale, the associated closing ratio, and the sales cycle, a monthly average sales revenue would equal $15,735. What should be compared at this point is the amount of sales revenue per period required by the organization and your personal revenue goal. Comparing these figures to the calculation, a tactical plan can be developed to change any, or all, of the twelve factors to achieve the desired result.

In this real-world example, the organization's quota was $40,000 per month. If the monthly average sales revenue is $15,735, it creates a deficit of $24,265. Even before the first minute of the selling month begins, the Sales Professional can conclude that the elements of his sales activity must be altered or there will be absolutely no chance of achieving quota, not to mention any chance of making real money.

In this case, and what is common with sales-compensation plans, is that the quota is given a six-month ramp-up period to allow the Sales Professional time to build a customer base. This ramp-up required only a portion of the total to be achieved each month up to the sixth month. On month six, the total $40,000 quota would be the required level of sales revenue as well as the required level for each month moving forward. In this example, not only does the $40,000 quota have no chance of being achieved consistently each month in the initial six months of the ramp-up period, but it also has little chance of being achieved in the following six months and beyond. The key word is *consistently*. A satisfactory "hit" here or there can occur, but that would only be short-lived until the averages play out in the subsequent months. A common misinterpretation by Management is when that one "hit" occurs, it is attributed to some specific activity, rather than simply a random outcome. Then, that chosen activity would be pounced on and made a required activity for the rest of the sales team.

A sustainable level of production can be reached only after many, many accumulations of sales cycles until a multitude of closed sales occurs each month. But those results could counteract the previous deficits only through a long tenure on the job. Unfortunately, before that happens, you'd be poorly commissioned and résumé shopping.

In addition, in this scenario, the sales employee turnover was through the roof, and this was placed on the shoulders of the "failing" Sales Professionals and their inability to carry out the required prospecting methods. Management didn't blame poor selling technique, or poor closing ability, or even lack of product knowledge, which may or may not have contributed. Instead, the phrase I heard too many times was that the "failing" sales reps "really didn't want to work," as if they were throwing in the towel on their careers. The truth was, they didn't want to exhaust themselves with guaranteed futility. And that conclusion should have been deduced from the real data being carried around in the supervisors' pockets.

Take Your Time

If you're hyperventilating—or worse, intimidated—by this tool to the point where you're considering changing your profession from sales, don't. You may be thinking that the data necessary for completing the equation are too difficult to acquire, or the components in the equation are not something you've remotely thought about. Those concerns may be, and probably are, accurate, because until now you may have never even come close to ascertaining the production elements of your profession. So, let's slow down, take a step back, and learn the simple building blocks for compiling the proper metrics of Tactical Prospecting.

The Tactical Measurement of Tactical Prospecting

The philosophy behind Tactical Prospecting is to create a sales structure in which you can produce the most in the least amount of time. Not a revolutionary idea by itself, but the processes used to achieve this provide a new vision. The problem with typical sales metrics is that they are either a collection of data with no connection to the elements of accurate sales activity or they are placed within a lengthy time frame with a preset deadline that is somewhere way off into the future. In the beginning, there is complacency, and as the deadline gets closer, there is panic.

At first, the allotted time to reach your revenue goal seems endless. There's a new month with a new, far-off horizon. It's like winning a million-dollar lottery; first, there is overspending because the bucket of money seems more than would ever be needed, until you get closer to emptying the bucket, and then you become thrifty. With a monthly quota to reach, at the beginning of the month, there's a perception of an abundance of time to achieve the necessary objectives—for instance, appointments. And a percentage of these appointments will become sales. Then, as time in the month passes and you get closer to the deadline, there's ensuing pressure from a rush to perform. This becomes a vicious cycle month to month of complacency, then stress, disrupting normal sales momentum. As a result, it results in a recuperation period at the beginning of each new quota timeframe.

At the heart of this vicious cycle is the incorrect perception that there's an abundance of time until the end of the selling period.

By comparing one single objective—let's say, gaining a single appointment—to a new bucket of time—let's say, thirty days—the perceived level of production needed is vastly underestimated compared with the required level of production. And if the total number of necessary objectives is determined during the complacency period—for instance, twelve appointments in the thirty-day period—this will create a sense of panic as motivation but will offer nothing as a tactical plan to achieve the objectives. Then all you're left with is the "uh-oh" factor—*Uh-oh, only three weeks left. Uh-oh, I need four deals in the last week.* And this results in the comical three-step sales strategy: Step 1: Forecast, Step 2: Panic, Step 3: Excuses.

Since panic is a pretty good motivator but useless as a tactic, the methods of prospecting used to gain these appointments must be analyzed by their production value produced in the shortest amount of time, not the allowable amount of time. And that is a function of the Tactical Prospecting Mentality.

I'd like to point out a simple fact: all prospecting methods work. They can all succeed in gaining an appointment if the allowable time to do so is endless. And if the time is less than endless and there's a deadline, the methods can still produce appointments, but not enough of them.

The total allowable time period is irrelevant as a meter of production. What is essential is to view the production gained in the shortest amount of time as a unit of measurement. Which brings us to the three Tactical Prospecting measurement principles:

Principle 1: One Appointment—Collect data on the amount of time it takes to gain a single appointment.

Principle 2: Method Comparison—Compare the measurements of all prospecting activities.

Principle 3: Time Allocation—Identify and concentrate on the highest producing methods.

With knowledge of these principles, all that remains is figuring out how to acquire the metrics.

The Prospecting Productivity Index Equations

The Prospecting Productivity Index Equations are tools used to properly gauge the production value of your prospecting methods. They consist of four equations that determine, on a numerical basis, the resources expended to generate appointments, to sell those appointments, and the financial costs of each. They are employed to calculate index metrics for the Hourly Time to Appointment, the Hourly Time to a Sale, the Dollar Cost of an Appointment, and the Dollar Cost of a Sale.

The four equations are:

1. The Appointment Productivity Index

$$API = \frac{\text{Appointment Gained}}{\text{Hourly Investment of Time}}$$

The components of the equation are:

Appointments	Appt
Hourly Investment of Time	HIT

2. The Sales Productivity Index

$$SPI = \left(\frac{\text{Appointment Gained}}{\text{Hourly Investment of Time}} \right) * \text{Closing Ratio}$$

The components of the equation are:

Appointments	Appt
Hourly Investment of Time	HIT
Closing Ratio	CR

3. The Appointment Productivity Cost

$$APC = \frac{\text{Hourly Dollar Rate}}{\left(\dfrac{\text{Appointment Gained}}{\text{Hourly Investment of Time}}\right)}$$

The components of the equation are:

Appointments	Appt
Hourly Investment of Time	HIT
Hourly Dollar Rate	HR

4. The Sales Productivity Cost

$$SPC = \frac{\text{Hourly Dollar Rate}}{\left(\dfrac{\text{Appointment Gained}}{\text{Hourly Investment of Time}} * \text{Closing Ratio}\right)}$$

The components of the equation:

Appointments	Appt
Hourly Investment of Time	HIT
Closing Ratio	CR
Hourly Dollar Rate	HR

The Steps in Data Collection:

1. Record the number of attempts made to gain one appointment.
2. Calculate the number of hours to gain one appointment.
3. Determine the quality of the appointment by the closing ratio.
4. Determine the financial cost to generate one appointment.
5. Determine the financial cost to close one sale.

Real-World Prospecting Methods

I will compare three common prospecting methods: cold calling, professional telemarketing, and marketing. All three will then be compared with the Alliance Process.

Cold Calling

Cold calling encompasses all forms of this prospecting activity as a general category. These methods vary from telephone, in-person direct communication, or indirect correspondence, such as email. Although the methods vary, the cold-calling concept is the same: any activity attempting to gain an appointment with a prospect in which there was no prior knowledge or communication.

Professional Telemarketing

Professional telemarketing encompasses communicating with prospects for the Sales Professionals. They range from company-employed telemarketers to outsourced telemarketing organizations. Although there tends to be a higher success rate with direct employees than outsourced telephone cold callers, the category will include all types with a success rate with a combined average. Although any appointments gained in the scenario are transferred to the Sales Professional, the success ratio of the telemarketer themselves will be the analyzed metrics of this category.

Marketing

Marketing is used as a general term representing any prospecting activity conducted by some form of secondary entity which generates initial appointments. These prospects are then transferred to Sales Professionals for the next step in the prospecting process. The activities include all forms of media activity designed to generate an appointment—direct mailers, automated calls or emails, telemarketing activity both in-house and outsourced, and virtually any other prospecting activity conducted by a secondary party. The difference is that these metrics are analyzed by the results of the second step in the prospecting process, after the prospect appointment has been transferred to the Sales Professional and further pursued by them.

Experiential Data

I've used the data compiled in my career, which includes my personal prospecting results, what I've calculated from organizations' data, and the metrics generated from other individual Sales Professionals. The data achieved through the Alliance Process are my own; however, data from your own similar methods can be substituted. Now is the time to be fair to yourself and use truly accurate data! No one is watching.

How Many Hours Does It Take to Generate an Appointment?

The Appointment Productivity Index

The Appointment Productivity Index is a measurement of the time invested to generate a single appointment. In addition to determining the time spent with an individual prospecting method, the index measurement can be used as a comparison against other methods that are currently or potentially used. Practically speaking, a minimum of one month's worth of data should be acquired before finalizing any determination. With less than that, it's common to produce skewed results of both high and low ratios of success.

> 1. **Hourly time to appointment.**
> 2. Hourly time to sale.
> 3. Financial cost of appointment.
> 4. Financial cost of sale.

The Appointment Productivity Index Equation (API):

$$API = \frac{Appointment\ Gained}{Hourly\ Investment\ of\ Time}$$

How Does the Time of Each Prospecting Method Compare?

1. Cold-Calling API Data:

Total hours expended to generate one appointment:

Appointments	1
Total Hours	8

$$API = \frac{1\ Appointment}{8\ Hours} = 0.125$$

What does this mean?

Well, 0.125 appointments is gained for each prospecting hour of time. That figure represents one-eighth of an appointment for each prospecting hour of work. Or, in a more typical form, this prospecting method will on average require 8 hours of prospecting to achieve 1 appointment. Well, that measurement is a powerful representation of the effort required with this method, but what is a real eye-opener is when that index is compared with the yield from the other methods.

2. Professional Telemarketing API Data:

Total hours expended to generate one appointment:

Appointments	1
Total Hours	4

$$API = \frac{1\ Appointment}{4\ Hours} = 0.25$$

The API translates into one-fourth of an appointment for every prospecting hour or one appointment for every four hours of telemarketing. It makes sense that Professional Telemarketers exhibit a greater proficiency level than a Sales Professional, and as a result, exhibit double the success rate of Sales Professionals.

3. Marketing API Data:

The data used in the following equation is derived from the appointments that are provided to the Sales Professional, which were originally gained through some form of secondary entity. Since these methods are initiated by an intermediary party such as a marketing department or a telemarketing company and transferred to the Sales Professional, the data generated from the Sales Professional's success at finalizing the appointment are put into the equation. For instance, a telemarketer may make two hundred calls in a week and produce five appointments. Those five appointments would be transferred to the appropriate Sales Professional and the results of their follow-up calls to finalize the meeting are the data used in the analysis. Since much less time is used to confirm a meeting with the five appointments, there will be less investment of time by the Sales Professional than the marketing entity. Not all prospects will follow through with an appointment—some will cancel, or not show up—in which case the number of appointments gained from the original five appointments is the data used in the "Appt" portion of the equation.

Total hours expended to generate one appointment:

Appointments	1
Total Hours	.5

$$API = \frac{1\ \text{Appointment}}{.5\ \text{Hours}} = 2.0$$

In this case, the extrapolated data shows that 2 appointments will be made with each prospecting hour or half hour to gain one appointment that was generated by some form of marketing and transferred to the Sales Professional. Comparing the two methods of prospecting conducted specifically by Sales Professionals, the index numbers are 0.125 and 2. This data reveals that having a marketing entity conduct the initial prospecting activity will yield a productivity level 16 times greater than having Sales Professionals cold call for themselves. I intentionally did not average the data from both the marketing entity and the Sales Professional, which could be done to determine a combined API. At this level, the Sales Professional should focus only on the data generated through their own efforts.

A Comparison of the Three Methods API:

Sales Professional Cold-Calling	0.125 hour
Telemarketer	0.250 hour
Marketing Transferred Appointments	2.0 hours

4. **Alliance Process API Data:**

Total hours expended to generate one appointment:

Appointments	1
Total Hours	.33

$$API = \frac{1 \text{ Appointment}}{.33 \text{ Hours}} = 3.0$$

Since this process does not involve a machine-like, repetitive, raw number of attempts, the data is an average across all **Tactical Prospecting** activity, which includes the appointments gained through the near-zero-net time output of the Alliance Process. We can see that there is tremendous productivity advantage utilizing the Alliance Process compared with the common methods. The process yields an API of three, or three appointments for every prospecting hour. On average, one appointment is made for every

> **Tactical Prospecting:** creating a structure to identify Opportunities in the shortest time possible.

twenty minutes of invested time! The chart below clearly shows the productivity comparison between the various prospecting methods. Remember that the higher the Index, the more productive is the method.

Method	Invested Time to Gain 1 Appointment	API
Sales Professional Cold Calling	8 hours	0.125
Professional Telemarketer	4 hours	0.250
Marketing	0.5 hour (30 minutes)	2.0
Alliance Process	0.33 hour (20 minutes)	3.0

The graph below reveals the API comparisons:

Appointment Productivity Index

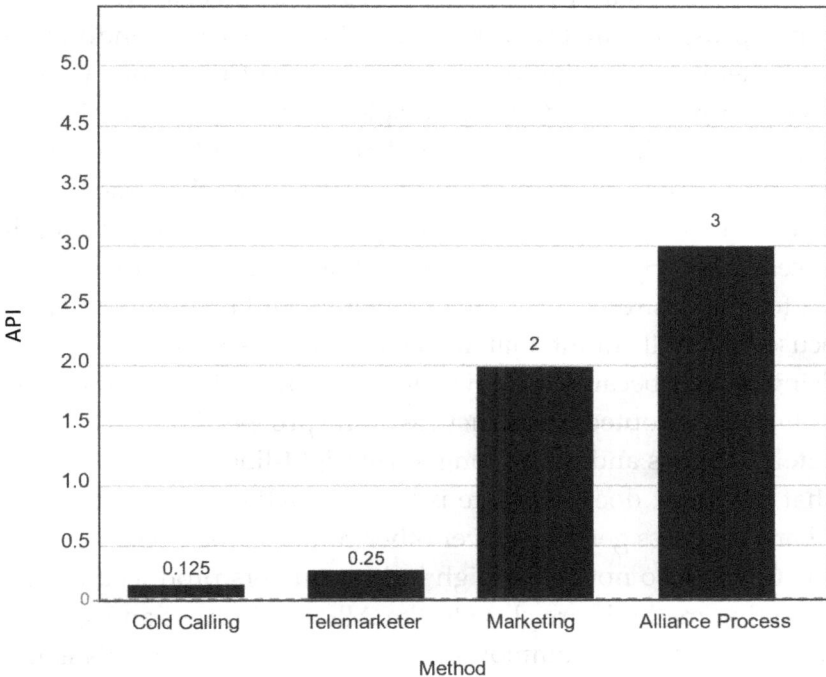

And the direct comparison between the most- and least-productive methods:

Method	API
Sales Professional Cold Calling	0.125
Alliance Process	3.000

API Comparison: 3 / 0.125 = 24

You can see that there is an immense difference in productivity levels associated with each method. The Alliance Process is twenty-four times more productive than cold calling, or 2,400 percent. However, the tremendous productivity advantage cannot be viewed as a direct comparison to standard prospecting. The difference is in the methodology. The appointments are made with prospects that already want to meet, even before you've communicated with them.

Your individual metrics may differ due to your abilities at performing the components of the prospecting that generate the data. For instance, you may not be able to research and call ten telemarketing prospects in thirty minutes. Proficiencies of individual components can be the focus of improvement until they're perfected within the foundation principle of Tactical Prospecting.

Also, the high or low index numbers don't imply that all other methods should be discarded. I've found that they each have value and, in many ways, feed off each other to produce an overall success level. However, the method that achieves the highest index for the desired goal is the one that should be predominantly focused on. I'll admit that using a comparison index is a bit disingenuous because I know that once the Alliance Process is proficiently adopted, the structure of the prospecting world completely changes and it's no longer a straight-line comparison. But what the index does illustrate is the productivity power that the Alliance Process generates over other common methods.

You may also notice the high index numbers produced by the marketing methods are close to the Alliance Process and greatly surpasses the more common methods. The reason for this is the way they relate to the time expended by the individual Sales Professional, regardless of the origin. In these situations, the initial labor is expended by an intermediary party and the time wasted on failing attempts is not expended by the Sales Professional. The "misses" are weeded out by someone else. The speed to appointment is the first part of the process. The quality of the appointment is then determined by the closing ratio associated with each method.

What Percentage of Appointments Close a Sale?

The Sales Productivity Index

The Sales Productivity Index equation is the next step in the analysis and probably the most telling piece of data. It is a quality metric added to the equation in the form of the closing ratio of the appointments. The initial goal of prospecting is, of course, gaining the appointment; however, it has

1. Hourly Time to appointment.
2. Hourly time to sale.
3. Financial cost of appointment.
4. Financial cost of sale.

become more accepted as the only goal. The quality of the appointment is the key and overshadows total number of appointments. Again, as the closing ratio of an appointment is a characteristic of the prospecting method, it is also, to a lesser extent, a result of other variables, *the least of which is the closing ability of the Sales Professional!* That's right, the closing ability of the Sales Professional is dependent on the multitudinous characteristics of the prospect, the negotiating ability of both the Sales Professional, and the prospect and the competence level of all the non-sales functions within your own organization. And of all these, the Sales Professional's negotiation ability is the only variable under their own control.

The Sales Productivity Index Equation (SPI):

$$SPI = \left(\frac{Appointment\ Gained}{Hourly\ Investment\ of\ Time} \right) * Closing\ Ratio$$

Now let's take it to the next level and include the closing percentages of the methods and determine an SPI for each. One key point to remember is that this measurement indicates the percentage of appointments that are ultimately sold, regardless of the timeframe. For the purposes of gauging prospecting productivity, the closing rate is a function of the prospecting timeframe, not the sales-cycle timeframe.

How Do the Closing Percentages of Each Prospecting Method Compare?

1. Cold-Calling SPI Data: A 10 percent Closing Ratio

Total hours expended to generate one appointment	
Appointments	1
Total Hours	8
Closing Ratio	0.1

$$SPI = \left(\frac{1 \text{ Appointment}}{8 \text{ Hours}} \right) * 0.1 = 0.0125$$

What does this mean?

There will be 0.0125 appointments sold for each prospecting hour of time. That figure represents about 1/80 of a sale for each prospecting hour of work. In a more practical expression, this prospecting method will on average take 80 hours to achieve 1 sale. That measurement is a powerful representation of the effort required, but what may be surprising is that index compared with the yield from the other methods.

2. **Professional Telemarketers SPI Data: A 10 percent Closing Ratio**

Total hours expended to generate one appointment	
Appointments	1
Total Hours	4
Closing Ratio	0.1

$$SPI = \left(\frac{1 \text{ Appointment}}{4 \text{ Hours}}\right) * 0.1 = 0.025$$

What does this mean?

The SPI of 0.025 equals 1/40 of a sale for every prospecting hour or 1 sale for every 40 hours of telemarketing.

3. **Marketing SPI Data: A 20 percent Closing Ratio**

Total hours expended to generate one appointment	
Appointments	1
Total Hours	0.5
Closing Ratio	0.2

$$SPI = \left(\frac{1 \text{ Appointment}}{0.5 \text{ Hour}}\right) * 0.2 = 0.4$$

What does this mean?

It would take half an hour to communicate with these prospects by the salesperson and has a closing ratio of 20 percent. This method will yield a SPI of 0.4. That means 2/5 of a sale will be made with each prospecting hour or 2.5 prospecting hours are required to close 1 sale in which the appointment was generated by marketing and transferred to the Sales Professional.

Comparing two methods of prospecting—professional telemarketing and marketing—the index numbers are 0.0125 and 0.4. Having the marketing entity prospect for appointments and provide those appointments to the salesperson yields a productivity level 32 times greater than having salespeople call for themselves.

4. Alliance Process SPI Data: A 65 percent Closing Ratio

As the API for Allies yields a much greater appointment success rate than the other methods, the quality of these appointments is also vastly superior. As a result, the closing ratio of 65 percent is primarily due to the characteristics of the Tactical Prospecting Process and less due to the ancillary variables, *especially* the selling abilities of the Sales Professional.

Total hours expended to generate one appointment	
Appointments	1
Total Hours	0.33
Closing Ratio	0.65

$$SPI = \left(\frac{1 \text{ Appointment}}{0.33 \text{ Hour}}\right) * 0.65 = 1.95$$

We can see that there is a tremendous productivity advantage when utilizing the Alliance Process compared with the common methods. With Allies, 1.95 sales are closed for each hour of prospecting. On average, 1 sale is closed every 30 minutes of prospecting time. The following chart clearly shows the productivity comparison between the various prospecting methods.

METHOD	EXPENDED TIME TO CLOSE ONE APPOINTMENT	API	SPI
Sales Professional Cold-Calling	8 Hours	0.125	0.0125
Professional Telemarketer	4 Hours	0.25	0.025
Marketing	0.5 Hour (30 minutes)	2.0	0.4
Alliance Process	0.33 Hour (20 minutes)	3	1.95

Sales Productivity Index

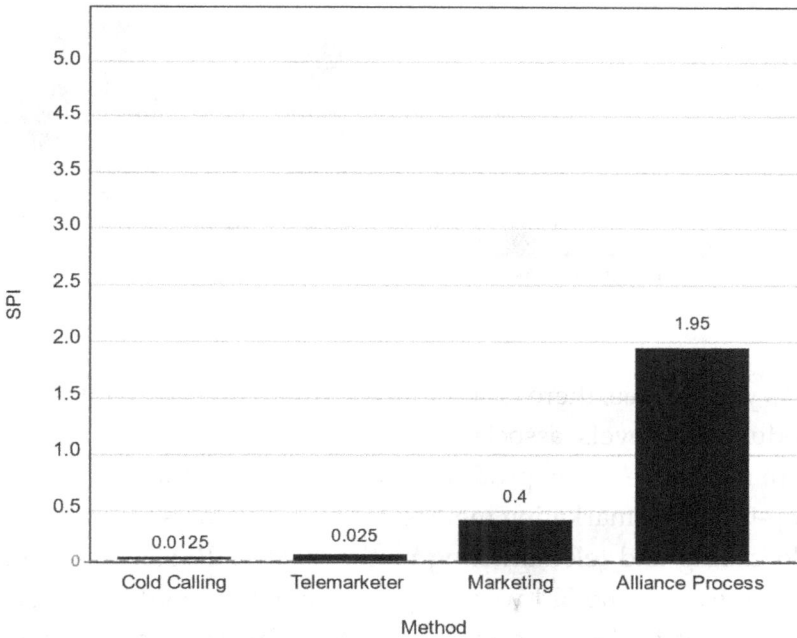

The importance of the Sales Productivity Index for each pro-specting method is that it's a true representative value index of your profession. There may be methods that produce a high index number for appointments gained, but appointments alone are not the final objective with prospecting. The goal is to gain the sale, and if a method provides only a high success rate of appoint-ments, its productivity value can be misleading. The strategic con-clusion may be to employ that method too long. This is illustrated by comparing the methods' API to their respective SPI:

Appointment/Sales Productivity Comparison Index

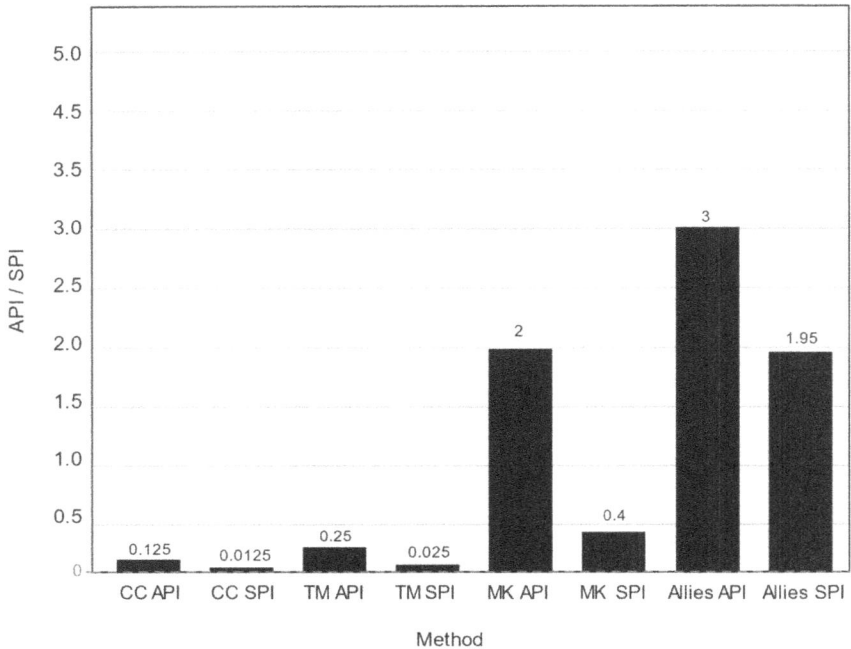

As you can see, there is an immense difference in the total sales productivity levels associated with each method. But what is more indicative of the productivity disparities is the tremendous drop-off of the marketing method from its API to its SPI. With the cold-calling and telemarketing methods, the API starts out very low, so even if the SPI weren't proportional, it wouldn't be surprising that it also produced a low SPI. But the marketing SPI drop-off to one-fifth of its API shows the resulting poor-selling quality of the appointments produced by that method.

Also, the marketing method API starts out at a strong productivity level equal to 66 percent of the Alliance Process API, but its SPI only produces a mere 20 percent of the Alliance Process SPI. And comparing best with worst, the Alliance Method is 156 times more productive than cold calling, or more than 15,000 percent.

Method	
Alliance SPI Index	1.95
Telemarketing SPI Index	0.0125

SPI Comparison: 1.95 / 0.0125 = 156

This data may differ when compared with your own personal assessments. The differences between the indexes attained through your own prospecting methods may not stand out as much. That's okay. As I mentioned earlier, through no fault of your own, the prospecting method that you considered networking, or any other method for that matter, was probably not similar to the process described as Allies. I'm sure that at some time in your career you were referred a prospect by a close friend or colleague and it became a quick closed sale. Examine the life cycle of that prospect and compare the results with those gained through one week's worth of telemarketing. Although your results may not be close to the data shown here, it will still show a glaring difference. And it will show what the future can hold.

How Much Does It Cost to Gain an Appointment?

As a Sales Professional, it is important to be aware of negative prospecting factors within your selling organization. As many procedures and subsequent costs can be influenced by you indirectly, they can absolutely control you directly. The consequences may not appear right away, but they will eventually. Therefore, while trying to answer the question *How much will I earn?* you must also be aware of the costs to your organization.

Prospecting Productivity Cost

As a next step in the analysis, the Prospecting Productivity Cost determines the value of a prospecting method as a function of dollar cost to produce the appointment and to produce the sale. The cost is determined by the individual sales prospector's hourly guaranteed pay but can also be a Target dollar amount. The Target is usually a quota amount but can be any potential revenue goal. The Target revenue values are best used as comparison measurements, because if they are a goal amount that can't be achieved using a certain prospecting method, this can accurately illustrate the accumulation of unattained potential revenue. For instance, if the Target revenue is a monthly quota, that unattained level will accumulate in each of the selling periods that follow, creating an unscalable mountain of negative revenue production.

1. Hourly Time to appointment.
2. Hourly Time to sale.
3. Financial cost of appointment.
4. Financial cost of sale.

The Appointment Productivity Cost Equation (APC):

$$APC = \frac{HR}{API}$$

Hourly Dollar Rate (HR): the per-hour dollar cost paid to the Sales Professional **prospector**.

The Sales Productivity Cost Equation (SPC):

$$SPC = \frac{HR}{SPI}$$

The Prospecting Productivity Cost Index would ideally be the lowest possible number, whereas the Prospecting Productivity Index would ideally be the highest. As a Sales Professional, it is important to be aware of the quality of the methods as they relate to the Target revenue investment. The hourly dollars could be any form of financial investment as well: hourly salary, marketing dollars, or opportunity-cost dollars. Just as your success depends on closed sales, it also depends on the costs incurred by your organization. Unfortunately, I have experienced the demise of too many companies that haphazardly spent millions on appointment-generating services that made money for the intermediary marketing companies but ultimately doomed the organizations and the Sales Professionals.

The Appointment Productivity Cost Components

Hourly Dollar Rate (HR):	This is the hourly dollar rate for the specific prospecting method.
Appointment Productivity Index (API):	The amount of time to gain one appointment.

The Appointment Productivity Cost Equation:

$$APC = \frac{\text{Hourly Dollar Rate}}{\text{Appointment Productivity Index}}$$

What Are the Appointment Cost Comparisons of Each Method?

1. Sales Professional Cold-Calling APC Example Data:

The Sales Professional earning $80,000 per year has prorated earnings of $38 per hour. Dividing the hourly rate by the telemarketing API of 0.125 produces an APC of $304. This means that the appointment productivity cost to generate one appointment by a Sales Professional is $304.

Annual Salary	$80,000
Hourly Rate	$38
API	0.125
APC	$304

$$APC = \frac{\$38}{0.125} = \$304$$

2. Professional Telemarketers APC Example Data:

The Professional Telemarketer earning $30,000 per year has prorated earnings of $14 per hour. Dividing the hourly rate by the telemarketing API of 0.25 produces an APC of $56. This means that the appointment productivity cost to generate one appointment by a Professional Telemarketer is $56.

Annual Salary	$30,000
Hourly Rate	$14
API	0.25
APC	$56

$$APC = \frac{\$14}{0.25} = \$56$$

3. Marketing APC Example Data:

The Sales Professional's salary of $80,000 and hourly rate of $38 is used in the example since they're receiving appointments generated by a marketing intermediary. The API of the marketing intermediary is also used in the calculation. Since this productivity index is greater than the telemarketing API, the cost per appointment is much lower.

Annual Salary	$80,000
Hourly Rate	$38
API	2
APC	$19

$$APC = \frac{\$38}{2} = \$19$$

4. Alliance Process APC Example Data:

The Sales Professional's salary of $80,000 is a prorated hourly rate of $38. Dividing the hourly rate by the Allies API of 3 generates an APC of $12. This means that the appointment productivity cost to generate one appointment by a salesperson using the Alliance Process is $12.

Annual Salary	$80,000
Hourly Rate	$38
API	3
APC	$12

$$APC = \frac{\$38}{3} = \$12$$

A comparison of the least- and most-productive methods performed by the same Sales Professional also provides a revealing comparison of the respective costs:

	Salesperson Cold-Calling	Alliance Process
Annual Salary	$80,000	$80,000
Hourly Dollar Rate	$38	$38
API	0.125	3.000
APC	$304	$12

Cold calling compared with the Alliance Process:
APC = $304 compared to $12

In this scenario, cold calling is 25 times, or 2500 percent, costlier than the Alliance Process for gaining an appointment. Adding the APC to the original API list makes the scenario crystal clear. Even if it's not your money, wouldn't the methods deserve at least some type of investigation?

Method	API	APC
Salesperson Cold Calling	0.125	$304
Professional Telemarketer	0.250	$56
Marketing	2.0	$19
Alliance Process	3.0	$12

Appointment Productivity Cost

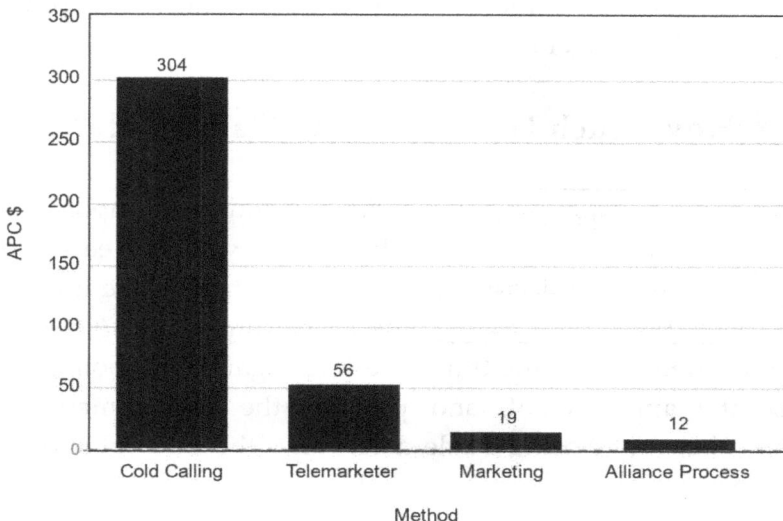

The Prospecting Productivity Equations should answer the question: How much will I earn?

There may be an obvious issue when reviewing Productivity Cost Indexes. Of course, when there is a high salary level, divided by a low Prospecting Index, the cost index, or cost per sale, will be very high. My warning is that the solution is not to lower the salary but to increase the productivity. This may seem obvious on the surface, but it isn't in practice. I have found that the higher a Sales Professional's salary, the more they are required to engage in the lower-productivity prospecting methods, with Management's constant reminder, "That's what the salary is for." And too often, what follows is the supervisor's decision is to cut the Sales Professional's compensation to bring it in line with their seemingly poor performance. The Productivity Cost Index is designed to be the wake-up call for both the Sales Professional and their supervisors.

As I mentioned earlier, it is disingenuous to try and compare the typical methods with the Alliance Process, as it completely changes the thinking. I don't want to say that Tactical Prospecting and the Alliance Process revolutionize prospecting. True networking has existed for years as a base form of Tactical Prospecting but has been avoided for a multitude of unjustified reasons. What is revolutionary is that the comparative data proves it's just plain negligent to dismiss it.

How Much Does It Cost to Gain a Sale?

1. Hourly Time to appointment.
2. Hourly Time to sale.
3. Financial cost of appointment.
4. Financial cost of sale.

Finally, and most importantly, what is the value of each prospecting method as the ultimate cost of closing a sale? Now that we have determined the time invested to gain an appointment, close the appointment, and pay for the appointment, the financial cost of closing a sale determines the true value of the appointment.

Sales Productivity Cost Components:

Hourly Dollar Rate (HR):	The per-hour dollar cost paid to the Sales Professional prospector.
Sales Productivity Index (SPI):	The metric signifying the quality of an appointment.

$$SPC = \frac{Hourly\ Dollar\ Rate}{Sales\ Productivity\ Index}$$

Sales Cost Method Comparisons

1. Cold Calling SPC Example Data:

The salesperson earning $80,000 per year prorates to $38 per hour. Dividing the hourly rate by the cold-calling SPI of 0.0125 produces an SPC of $3,040. This means that the cost to generate one sale by a salesperson engaging in cold calling is $3,040.

Annual Salary	$80,000
Hourly Rate	$38
SPI	0.0125
SPC	$3,040

$$SPC = \frac{\$38}{0.0125} = \$3,040$$

2. Professional Telemarketers SPC Example Data:

The Professional Telemarketer earning $30,000 per year pro rates to $14 per hour. Dividing the hourly rate by the telemarketing SPI of 0.025 produces an SPC of $560. This means that the cost to generate one sale by a Professional Telemarketer is $560.

Annual Salary	$30,000
Hourly Rate	$14
SPI	0.025
SPC	$560

$$SPC = \frac{\$14}{0.025} = \$560$$

3. Marketing SPC Example Data:

The salesperson's hourly rate is now divided by the SPI of transferred appointments. So, with an annual salary of $80,000 and an hourly rate of $38, the hourly rate is divided by the SPI of 0.4. This will result in a cost of $95 to gain a sale.

Annual Salary	$80,000
Hourly Rate	$38
SPI	0.4
SPC	$95

$$SPC = \frac{\$38}{0.4} = \$95$$

4. Alliance Process SPC Example Data:

The salesperson's hourly rate of pay of $38 divided by the Alliance Process SPI of 1.95 generates an SPC of $19.

Annual Salary	$80,000
Hourly Rate	$38
SPI	1.95
SPC	$19

$$SPC = \frac{\$38}{1.95} = \$19$$

Comparing the four methods:

Method	SPI	SPC
Salesperson Cold Calling	0.0125	$3,040
Professional Telemarketer	0.025	$560
Marketing	0.40	$95
Alliance Process	1.95	$19

Sales Productivity Cost

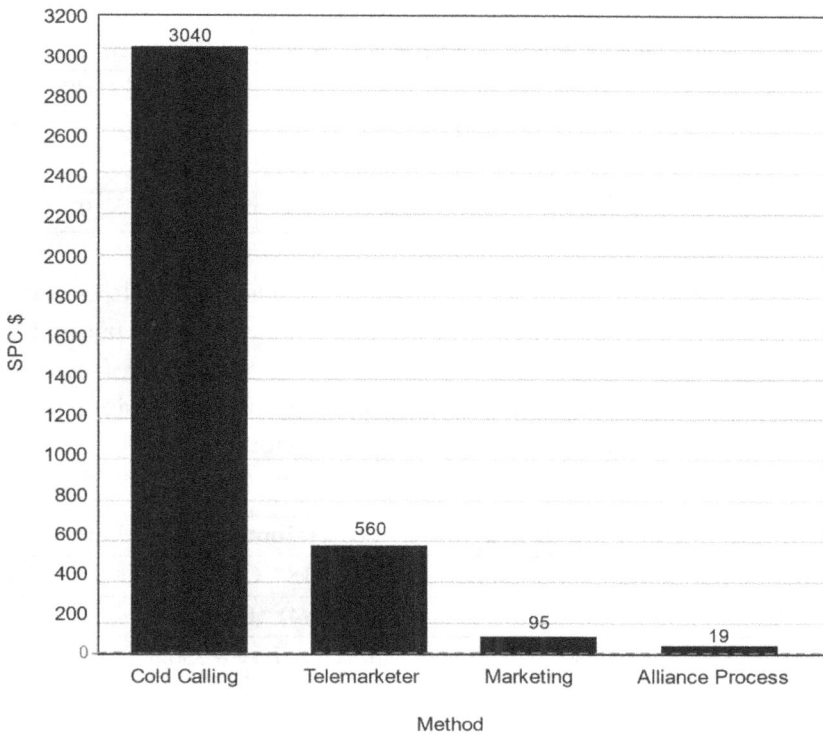

And by comparing the lowest-producing method of cold calling with the highest-producing Alliance Process, the cost divergence is immense:

	Salesperson Cold-Calling	Alliance Process
Annual Salary	$80,000	$80,000
Hourly Dollar Rate	$38	$38
SPI	0.0125	1.95
SPC	$3040	$19

SPC = $3040 compared with $19

$3040/$19 = 160 times greater

Cold calling is 160 times costlier than the Alliance Process at generating a sale, an "off-the-charts" percent. Finally, placing together all the index values provides a side-by-side comparison of the typical prospecting methods with the Alliance Process:

Method	API	SPI	APC	SPC
Salesperson Cold Calling	0.125	0.0125	$304	$3,040
Professional Telemarketer	0.250	0.025	$56	$560
Marketing	2.000	0.400	$19	$95
Alliance Process	3.000	1.950	$12	$19

After examining the metrics, wouldn't these methods deserve comparative analysis on a continual basis? Even by using the equations to analyze the two typical methods, Professional Telemarketers, and cold calling, wouldn't the conclusions warrant a change in tactics, or at least a discussion?

Salesperson Cold Calling	Professional Telemarketing
SPI = API * CR	SPI = API * CR
SPI = (1/8) * 0.1 = 0.0125	SPI = (1/4) * 0.1 = 0.025
Annual Salary = $80,000	Annual Salary = $30,000
Hourly Dollar Rate = $38	Hourly Dollar Rate = $14
SPC = $38/0.0125 = $3,040	SPC = $14/0.025 = $560

A Sales Productivity Cost of $3,040 compared with $560 or more than five times greater to have Sales Professionals cold calling rather than have the Professional Telemarketers perform that initial prospecting work. Now, I don't want to venture off into the sales-consulting arena, however, since we are not CFOs, we have the luxury of taking a leap of faith with the dollar values and making assumptions. So, let's assume that these Sales Productivity Costs are hard-cost dollars going out the door. At $3,040 minus $560, there would be $2,480 in savings. Assuming that the prospecting time is all also accurate, one telemarketing sale is closed on average for every 40 hours of prospecting time. If $2,480 is saved every 40 hours, or about $129,000 per year, those savings could now pay for any combination of new sales-production mechanisms: extra sales employees, four more Professional Telemarketers, or a combination of both. Maybe raise the Sales Professionals' salary and eliminate commission altogether. Okay, I may have ventured off a bit too far with that one—you may not be ready. With any of these additions, the sales production would increase, which creates more Opportunities, and on, and on. Now that's a spigot that should be turned on.

The Prospecting Productivity Equations are used to isolate the productivity levels of various prospecting methods and give the Sales Professional a head-start in ascertaining the prospecting productivity production in the necessary timeframe. The indices and revenue figures provide a basic snapshot of the level of production. By providing a numeric value to specific units of time, it quantifies what Sales Professionals have been sensing.

As the index data is accumulated, it will put into focus the origin of the frustration with standard methods of prospecting and their resulting sales productivity. The next step is to engage in a further in-depth analysis of the benefits and obstacles encountered during a Sales Professional's movement toward the ultimate result of the sale. The next step is to calculate momentum.

CHAPTER 11

How Much Am I
Being Forced to Earn?

Sales Prospecting Momentum

THE CONCEPT OF SALES Prospecting Momentum determines a value of movement through a time period as a result of engaging in a certain activity. The analyzed activity may or may not be related to sales prospecting but is viewed solely as its direct effect on your sales prospecting production. Any activity in which a Sales Professional engages will have a direct effect on their prospecting. Whether the activity is chosen or imposed, the resulting revenue calculation can be predetermined and compared with the potential sales revenue of other activities. For instance, if a Sales Professional is engaging in some practice that's producing twenty dollars per hour of sales revenue, that value can simply be the production measurement of an activity, a value compared with a target revenue goal, or the value compared with the revenue production of a separate activity.

The advantage of engaging in Prospecting Momentum analysis is that the Sales Professional is forced to conduct two underused but necessary practices. The first is engaging in the behavior of analysis itself. This obligates the Sales Professional to form the required habit of accurately measuring their prospecting results. And the second is gauging a rate of success to ensure that the desired amount of prospecting revenue is being achieved in the allowable time.

The most valuable conclusions will be drawn by comparing the potential revenue gain against any, and all, mandatory tasks that may interrupt momentum. And the data should be plotted on a chart to visualize the projected progress against the actual progress.

As sales-revenue momentum is gained or lost, the value is a translated equivalence with prospecting time. Although the revenue momentum is the metric used in the Momentum Equations, revenue and time are inexorably linked. As one directly translates into the other, revenue and time have equal importance to the Sales Professional.

The Momentum Equations

1. The Prospecting Momentum Equation

$$PM = \$X * \left(\frac{Appt}{HIT} * CR \right) * TT$$

2. The Target Momentum Difference Equation

$$TMD = PM - (HRT * TT)$$

3. The Comparison Momentum Equation

$$CM = \$X * \left(\left(\overset{\text{New Task}}{\frac{Appt}{HIT} * CR} \right) - \left(\overset{\text{Existing Task}}{\frac{Appt}{HIT} * CR} \right) \right) * TT$$

The Components of the Equations:

New Task	The Newly Engaged Prospecting Method or Task
Existing Task	The Existing Prospecting Method or Task
HIT	Hourly Investment of Time to Gain One Appointment for a Prospecting Method or Task
CR	Closing Ratio of the Prospecting Method or Task
$X	Average Dollar Revenue Per Sale
TT	The Amount of Time Designated for Method or Task
HRT	The Hourly Dollar Revenue Target

The Prospecting Momentum Equation (PM)

$$PM = \$X * \left(\frac{Appt}{HIT} * CR\right) * TT$$

The Prospecting Momentum Equation is used to gauge a quantity of sales revenue movement gained or lost, in a specific time period, by utilizing a specific prospecting method. By incorporating the key factors necessary to determine prospecting productivity, a resulting hourly rate of movement toward a goal can be calculated. And more important than simply determining the quantity of movement, the metrics used in the equation can ascertain at the outset if certain prospecting methods will produce enough to achieve the goal. For instance, using the following data in the example:

> **PM** = Prospecting Momentum Equation
> **$X** = Average Revenue Sale
> **SPI** = $\left(\frac{Appt}{HIT} * CR\right)$
> **TT** = Task Time

$X	$10,000
Appt	1
HIT	4
CR	0.2
TT	10

$$PM = \$X * \left(\frac{Appt}{HIT} * CR\right) * TT$$

$$PM = \$10{,}000 * \left(\frac{1}{4} * 0.20\right) * 10$$

$$PM = \$10{,}000 * (0.25 * 0.20) * 10$$

$$PM = \$10{,}000 * (0.05) * 10$$

$$PM = \$500 * 10$$

$$= \$5{,}000 \text{ (per ten-hour day of Task Time)}$$

The resulting calculation reveals that by employing the specific prospecting method, on average $500 per hour in positive revenue movement, or $5,000 in a 10-hour day of Task Time. This doesn't mean that by using this prospecting method, you'll accumulate $5,000 in revenue by 6 p.m. on any specific day. What it does mean is that you can expect to accumulate $5,000 for each 10-hour day of sales activity. Comparing this with a required goal amount, you can determine if the quantity of movement is enough within the allowable time. If your revenue goal is $200,000 in 20 days, it won't be, but if your goal is to sell $80,000 or $100,000, then that prospecting method will be successful, provided that the entire ten hours are used to prospect.

With the following chart, you can visualize your rate of momentum and determine where you will be:

Prospecting Sales Momentum ($)

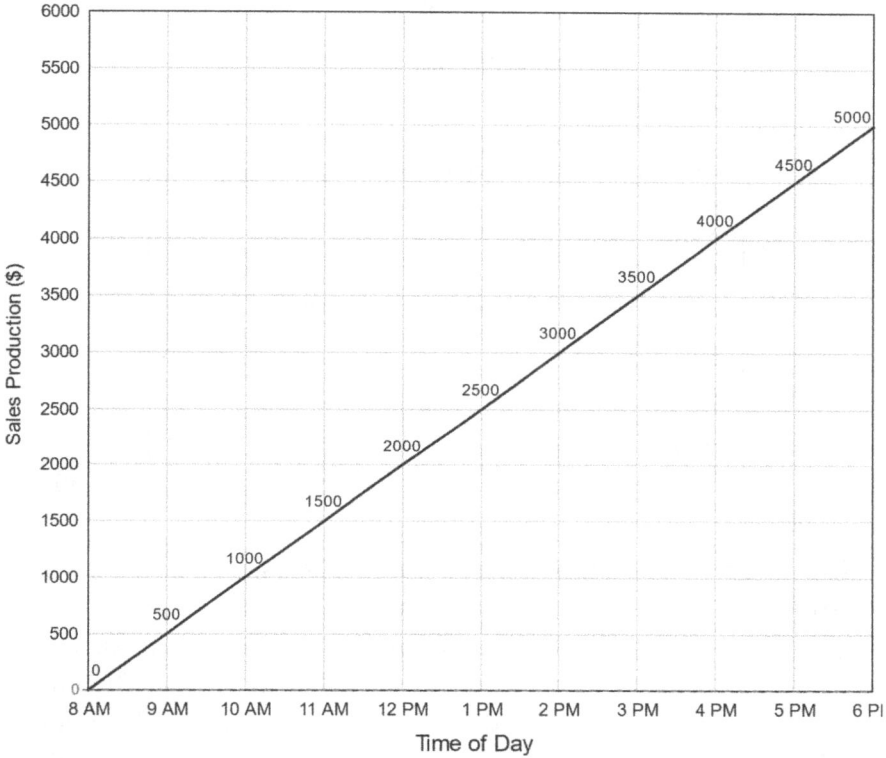

And to reiterate, the momentum of $500 in sales per hour is not meant to be a per-hour guarantee for any individual hour, although it can be. If a 10-day period of total revenue mo-

> **Momentum Equations:** equations that are designed to determine a rate of movement in sales revenue by employing a specific prospecting method.

mentum equals $50,000, you may have produced a "donut," a zero for the first week, then close 5 deals in week two. If the prospecting method metrics are accurate, then it will produce, on average, what it's supposed to, good or bad. What the momentum concept also provides is a feedback mechanism that can be used as a type of hourly meter to compare a revenue level against where your prospecting and deal activity is. But, if after the initial analysis, the momentum isn't where it's supposed to be, then a serious reevaluation of the prospecting method will be necessary.

The Target Momentum Difference Equation (TMD)

$$TMD = PM - (HRT * TT)$$

TMD = Target Momentum Difference
$X = Average Revenue per Sale
Appt = Appointment
HIT = Hourly Investment of Time per Appointment
CR = Sales Closing Rate of Appointment
$$SPI = \left(\frac{Appt}{HIT} * CR\right)$$
TT = Total Task Time of Activity

HRT = Hourly Revenue Target

The Target Momentum Difference Equation is used to calculate the difference between the quantity of sales revenue movement in a specific time period and the required revenue needed for the same period derived from a predetermined target value. The importance of determining the difference in the amount of movement is to calculate this value at the beginning of the time period, before engaging in the task. Then determine whether the Target can be achieved and the level of difference in the revenue movement. Use the data in this example.

$X	$10,000
Appt	1
HIT	4
CR	20%
TT	10 Hours
MONTHLY TARGET	$100,000
HOURS PER MONTH	173
HRT	$578

$$TMD = \left(\$X * \left(\frac{Appt}{HIT} * CR\right) * TT\right) - (HRT * TT)$$

$$TMD = \left(\$10{,}000 * \left(\frac{1}{4} * 0.20\right) * 10\right) - (\$578 * 10)$$

$$TMD = (\$10{,}000 * (0.25 * 0.20) * 10) - (\$5{,}780)$$

$$TMD = (\$10{,}000 * (0.05) * 10) - (\$5{,}780)$$

$$TMD = (\$500 * 10) - (\$5{,}780)$$

$$TMD = (\$5{,}000 - \$5{,}780)$$

$$TMD = -\$780 \text{ (per ten hour day)}$$

The calculation reveals a shortfall of $780 for the 10-hour period. Plot on the chart the Target Revenue Momentum amount broken out in the same time frame as the Prospecting Momentum Revenue amount.

Target Momentum Difference

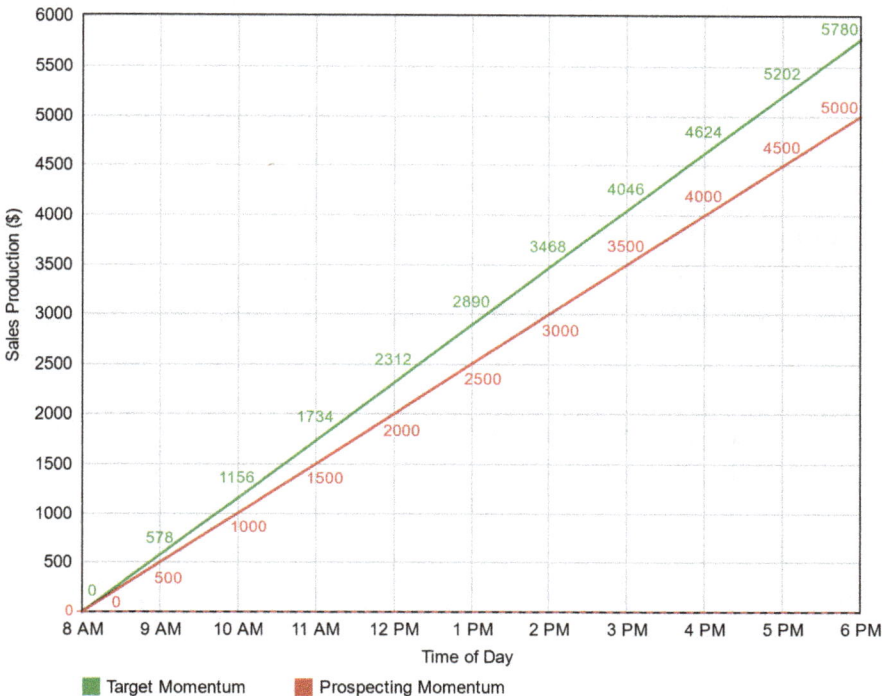

Target Momentum   Prospecting Momentum

With a Target momentum of $100,000 per month at 173 hours, for a 10-hour Task Time, the hourly momentum would equal $578 or $5,780 of Target momentum in a 10-hour period. The Prospecting Momentum will absolutely produce $5,000 in a 10-hour period, however, resulting in a deficit of $780 for each 10-hour period in which that prospecting method is used. As the trend line indicates, the momentum will be below the Target line and the Target will be missed. A new method will be required.

Comparison Momentum

The two key objectives of tracking your momentum are to ensure that the very act of data collection creates an awareness of your activity measurements, and as a feedback mechanism to ensure you remain on the proper trend to achieve the productivity goal. As the Prospecting Momentum tool provides insight into the basic factors of your revenue movement, as a powerful feedback tool, it measures the effects of disruption of the positive momentum.

I know first-hand the frustration of having a tactical sales plan ready for implementation, then being forced to engage in a completely different practice that disrupts my momentum. The reason for the frustration isn't simply a visceral response with no basis in your production. The feeling is based in an actual negative revenue momentum value that you've sensed but, until now, couldn't quantify.

Let's say that your Daily Momentum Chart shows stalled momentum, and by one p.m. you've returned from the twelve p.m. appointment, completely cognizant of the revenue level, and you're prepared to implement tactics to regain momentum. But then you get the "fire-drill" email from your supervisor, ordering everyone to return to the office at two p.m. for an unscheduled review, or sales meeting, or telemarketing blitz session. Regardless, if these tasks were scheduled or impulsive, they will create a continual decline in the momentum that is a quantifiable measurement staring you in the face. Now, by using the Comparison Momentum Equation, the origin of your frustration is calculable and as clear as day.

The Comparison Momentum Equation (CM)

New Task   Existing Task

$$CM = \$X * \left(\left(\frac{Appt}{HIT} * CR \right) - \left(\frac{Appt}{HIT} * CR \right) \right) * TT$$

The Comparison Momentum Equation calculates the loss or gain in prospecting momentum revenue by shifting from one task to another task. Some of the self-imposed tasks—such as experimenting with a new prospecting method, using new administrative processes, or even taking someone to lunch—can produce a positive or negative effect on momentum compared with the existing task in which you're presently engaged. The productivity potential of the new activity by itself isn't the most-significant factor. What's most significant is whether the new activity was forced on you or was voluntary. When tasks are imposed by Management with the intent of addressing sales behavior in some form—for example, a mandatory telemarketing session, a sales meeting, or a training session—you are stuck. You must ride it out, gritting your teeth and hoping it will ultimately provide an increased level of productivity value. However, if the new choice is voluntary, you can immediately assess its benefit and alter your choice with minimal loss or continue forward with positive gain.

The Components of the Equation:

CM	Comparison Momentum
$X	Average Revenue per Sale
New Task	The New Task
Appt	One Appointment for Newly Imposed Task (this can be zero for a non-prospecting task)
HIT	Hourly Investment in Time to Gain One Appointment for Newly Imposed Task (this can be zero for a non-prospecting task)
CR	Closing Ratio of a Sale (this can be zero for a non-prospecting task)
Existing Task	The Existing or Present Prospecting Task
Appt	One Appointment for the Existing Task
HIT	Hourly Investment in Time for the Existing Task
CR	Closing Ratio of a Sale for the Existing Task
TT	Task Time for the New Task

Using the data example:

$X	$10,000
New Task	Newly Imposed Prospecting Task
Appt	1 Appointment
HIT	8 Hours
CR	10%
Existing Task	Existing or Presently Engaged Prospecting Task
Appt	1 Appointment
HIT	4 Hours
CR	20%
TT	4 Hours

Let's input the data:

New Task	Existing Task

$$CM = \$X * \left(\left(\frac{\text{Appt}}{\text{HIT}} * CR \right) - \left(\frac{\text{Appt}}{\text{HIT}} * CR \right) \right) * TT$$

$$CM = \$10,000 * \left(\left(\frac{1}{8} * 0.10 \right) - \left(\frac{1}{4} * 0.20 \right) \right) * 4$$

$$CM = \$10,000 * \left((0.125 * 0.10) - (0.25 * 0.20) \right) * 4$$

$$CM = \$10,000 * \left((0.0125) - (0.05) \right) * 4$$

$$CM = \$10,000 * -0.0375 * 4$$

$$CM = -\$375 * 4 = -\$1,500$$

What the data shows is that by moving from your own prospecting task to, for example, a "Smile and Dial" telemarketing task, there will be, on average, a $375 loss of productivity per hour, or a total loss of $1,500 over the 4-hour Task Time. Now, what's most important is that these revelations can be gained only with a working knowledge of the metrics associated with each factor. Without that, all you're left with is a frustrated feeling that something isn't right and no evidence as to why. Even though you may see the small numerical gains on paper from a new prospecting task, it still may not justify what your gut is telling you: "I'm not gaining a little; I'm losing a lot." What will make it more apparent is to visualize on a graph the disruptive movement through your sales day:

Comparison Momentum

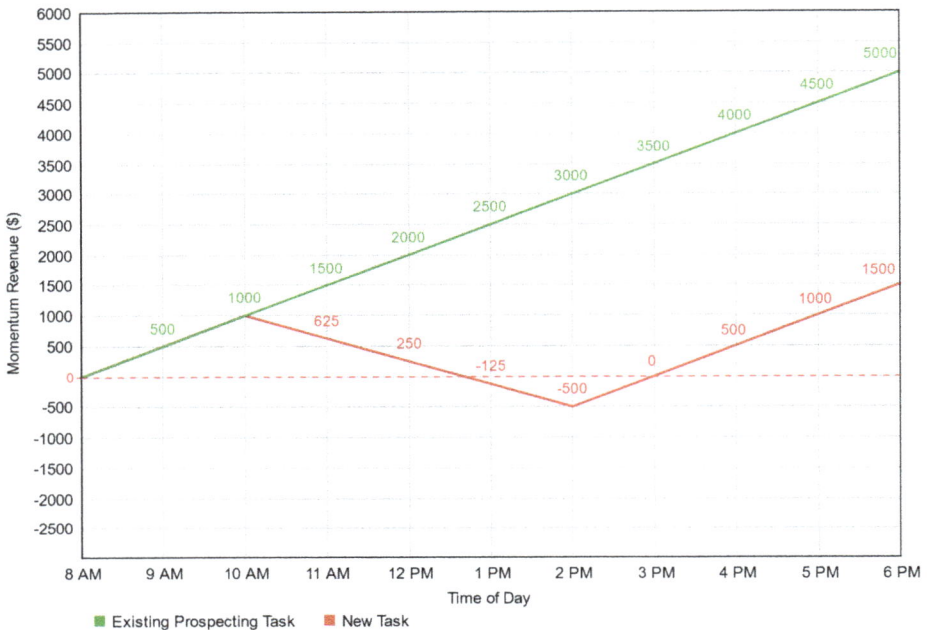

Chart: Comparison Momentum — X-axis: Time of Day (8 AM to 6 PM); Y-axis: Momentum Revenue ($), from -2500 to 6000.

Existing Prospecting Task values: 500, 1000, 1500, 2000, 2500, 3000, 3500, 4000, 4500, 5000

New Task values: 1000, 625, 250, -125, -500, 0, 500, 1000, 1500

Legend: ■ Existing Prospecting Task ■ New Task

By starting your day at 8 a.m. and engaging in your accepted, existing prospecting method that produces $500 per hour in momentum, by 10 a.m. the potential production reaches $1,000. Then you're required to return to the office and engage in Management's new prospecting method that potentially produces only $125 per hour. At 10 a.m., your momentum is broken and you go backward at a net-negative rate of $375 per hour—the $125 new level of production minus the $500 existing level of production. The disrupted momentum digs a hole of a negative $500 by 2 p.m. when the required task is complete. By 3 p.m., you're back on track, gaining $500 per hour. However, you're now at $0, the same level as seven hours earlier. It's as if you've expended a ton of effort up to that point and accomplished nothing for the day. By 3 p.m., there is a $3,500 deficit that you can never make up, unless you engage in a new prospecting method that produces more than $500 per hour. From a typical sales perspective, it's these disruptive tasks that create the deficit holes that carry over to the following quota periods. And when Management's justification for a specific task is the minimal amount of time involved—"It takes you only 4 hours a week"—you can see that the cost is a lot more than that.

It may appear that the amount of $500 per hour should be compared with a level of $125 per hour and plotted accordingly, as shown here.

Comparison Momentum

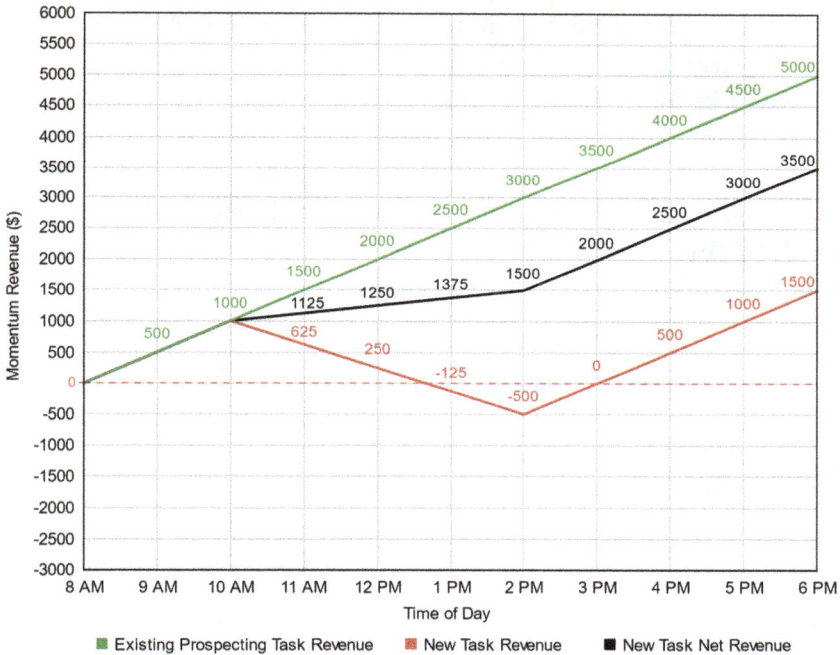

However, when conceptualizing Prospecting Momentum, revenue and time are mentally and physically joined. When the potential revenue is below what is expected to be produced, that quantity is equivalent to an equal quantity of time. If the New Task can produce a greater amount than the Existing Task, then the momentum toward the goal increases and you get there faster. But more often than not, the imposed New Task produces less, extending the time it takes to reach the goal. That increased time is lost. The more time lost, the further removed you are from the point in time when you changed tasks. It's like starting over because the tactical steps used with the Existing Task must be initiated all over again. And due to the length of disengagement, you may have to start from the absolute beginning, unable to pick up from where you left off. The prospecting advantages of information and communication have died on the vine. The physical, tactical, and psychological momentum has been disrupted, and the only question is by how much.

Revenue-Time

The net-revenue difference between both Tasks translates into net-prospecting time, and it's the quantity of that Revenue-Time that is paramount. For instance, if $1,000 of revenue has been anticipated by hour 2, and at that point the task changes, then the third, next hour will drop to a level of $625 of revenue momentum. If the difference between the revenue at hour 3—$1,500—is deducted from the momentum revenue, and that result is divided by the hourly revenue production of the Existing Task, then the time loss or gain can be determined.

Comparison Momentum

New Task Revenue: $125 per hour
Existing Task Revenue: $500 per hour
New Momentum Revenue: -$375 per hour

At 10 a.m.: New Task Point of Change Revenue is $1,000.
At 11 a.m.: Existing Task Revenue would be $1,500.
At 11 a.m.: New Momentum Revenue equals $625.

Equation: Existing Task Time Revenue – Momentum Revenue = Momentum Revenue Difference

or

Equation: $1,500 – $625 = $875

Existing Task Revenue Momentum per Hour

$$\frac{\$875}{\$500} = 1.75 \text{ hours}$$

Translated Prospecting Time: $875 / $500 = 1 ¾ hours, or ¾ longer to produce the same revenue as the Existing Task.

The chart shows an hourly comparison of Revenue Momentum viewed as time:

Revenue-Time Loss Chart

Time	Momentum Revenue	Actual Prospecting Time (HR)	Equivalent Momentum Prospecting Time (HR)	Net Time Loss/Gain (HR)
8:00 a.m.	$0	0	0	0
9:00 a.m.	$500	1	1	0
10:00 a.m.	$1,000	2	2	0
11:00 a.m.	$625	3	1.25	-1.75
12:00 p.m.	$250	4	0.5	-3.5
1:00 p.m.	-$125	5	-0.25	-5.25
2:00 p.m.	-$500	6	-1	-7
3:00 p.m.	$0	7	0	-7
4:00 p.m.	$500	8	1	-7
5:00 p.m.	$1,000	9	2	-7
6:00 p.m.	$1,500	10	3	-7

The chart shows that the relative time loss of seven hours stops at 3 p.m. However, unless the pace of the potential momentum revenue going forward is greater than $500 per hour, the seven hours of lost time can't be made up and the quota time period will maintain that time-production deficit. The concept of Sales Prospecting Momentum is viewed as a gain or loss of Revenue-Time as a result of altered tasks. If I can produce $500 in one hour but switch to a task that allows me to produce only $125 per hour, then the Momentum Revenue is -$375 for that hour. As this figure translates into my Revenue-Time, I am losing an additional ¾ of an hour per hour engaged in the new task.

To exhibit as clearly as possible the importance of focusing on the relative difference between the production potential from the Existing Task and New Task, view its effect on your Revenue-Time. The chart below shows the revenue of both Tasks on a monthly scale.

Comparison Momentum

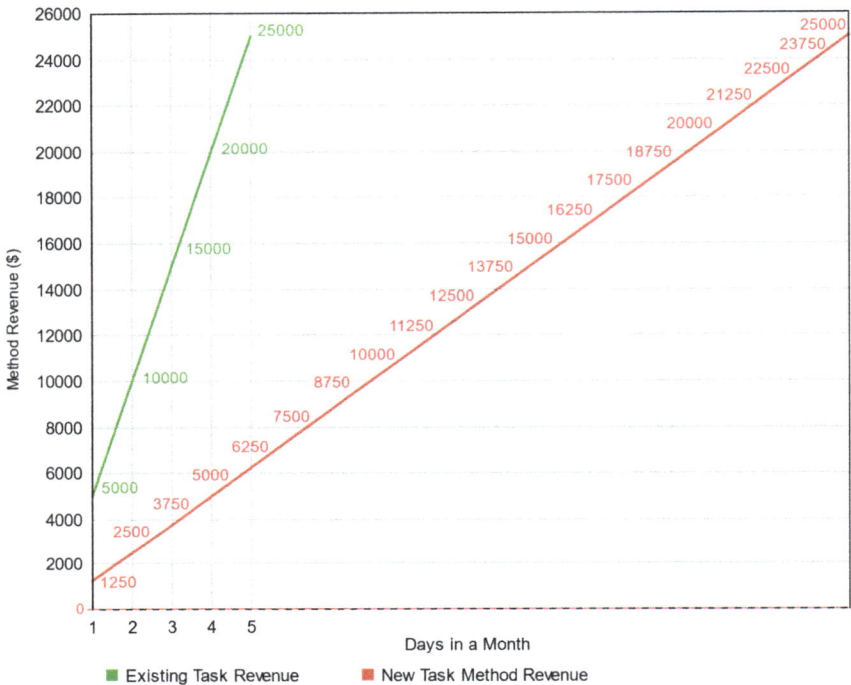

If the revenue of each method is extrapolated across a twenty-day month, the lower-producing New Task Method generates $25,000. However, compared with the Existing Task, $25,000 is generated after only one week.

If viewed from the different perspective of quantity of time, trading a greater producing method for a lesser producing one, it will take four times as long to gain an equal amount of revenue. But that's not all. What if the required task doesn't involve prospecting activity at all? As mentioned earlier, any task can create a disruption. Unfortunately, there has been a deluge of mandatory tasks imposed upon Sales Professionals for the good of some other alternative processes. Salespeople have become the test dummies for other employees' strategies. And regardless of the intent, the result is usually one-sided. The ideas can be as simple as more frequent sales meetings, additional administrative steps, or any extraneous new IT procedures; it doesn't matter. What matters is that if it's not a voluntary choice, then the precious time must be mentally tossed into the trash, sacrificed for the intended good of the salesperson.

Sometimes, there is that one-off procedure that really does help. Yes, some of those procedures do exist, however, they are a net benefit only because they waste a bit less time than the original procedure being replaced.

Listed here is a collection of tasks that, until now, have been relatively disassociated from potential sales productivity. However, if they're viewed within the concept of Sales Momentum, they take on different values. An example of these tasks has been assigned to the following graph. By incorporating the schedule of a Sales Professional's typical weekly activities, the Momentum Revenue can be plotted on a chart to visually represent the projected momentum versus the actual momentum.

If we calculated the production levels of these tasks compared with our existing level, assuming they provide little to no revenue, a week's worth of momentum may look like this:

Time	Monday	Tuesday	Wednesday	Thursday	Friday
8:00 a.m.	Drive Time	Drive Time	Drive Time	Appt	Normal Prospecting
9:00 a.m.	Sales Meeting	"Smile and Dial" Session	Role-Playing	Appt	Normal Prospecting
10:00 a.m.	Appt	"Smile and Dial" Session	Role-Playing	Normal Prospecting	Normal Prospecting
11:00 a.m.	Appt	"Smile and Dial" Session	Normal Prospecting	Normal Prospecting	Lunch
12:00 p.m.	Lunch	"Smile and Dial" Session	Normal Prospecting	Normal Prospecting	Review
1:00 p.m.	Normal Prospecting	Lunch	Lunch	Normal Prospecting	Normal Prospecting
2:00 p.m.	Normal Prospecting	Normal Prospecting	Normal Prospecting	Normal Prospecting	Normal Prospecting
3:00 p.m.	Normal Prospecting	Normal Prospecting	Normal Prospecting	Normal Prospecting	Normal Prospecting
4:00 p.m.	Normal Prospecting	Sales Administrative	Sales Administrative	Normal Prospecting	Sales Administrative
5:00 p.m.	Normal Prospecting	Sales Administrative	Sales Administrative	Normal Prospecting	Sales Administrative

Projected/Actual Prospecting Production Momentum

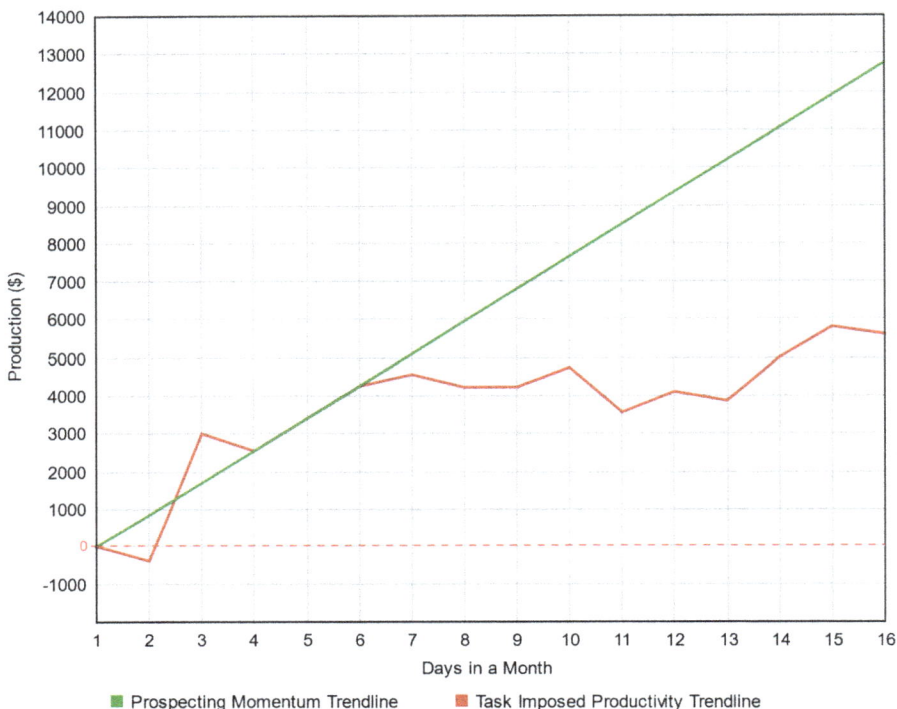

Comparing the red line—representing momentum of a typical salesperson's work week—with the green line—representing the prospecting momentum trend line—you can see the importance of deciding where to place your efforts. It's mind-blowing when you can finally put a quantifiable value on what your gut was telling you all along. It's not an insignificant amount of time to perform a mandatory task, as the imposers of those tasks would make you think. And those trainings or role-playing sessions probably didn't create the value that Management said they would. Of course, there are tasks that may be necessary, and I am not suggesting eliminating all processes that have a negative effect on prospecting productivity. That would not be realistic or even possible. However, knowing what effect these activities may have on sales productivity, wouldn't it make sense to transfer the wasteful ones from the Sales Professional and make the necessary ones as time efficient as possible?

At this point, you may have serious doubts about the production levels and metrics comparisons being proposed here. Maybe the figures shown by the Alliance Process seem unbelievably high and those of the standard methods seem unbelievably low. That's all okay. Questioning should be done continually as it relates to your profession. And as mentioned earlier, the production levels may vary, sometimes by a great deal according to each Sales Professional's ability. But ask yourself: Are you presently producing what's expected by you, or by your superiors? Are you achieving quota or any other sales goals on a continual basis? That's where the questioning should begin, and where the doubt should arise. The message may not be easy to accept. It's been said, "Don't blame the messenger," but it's time to start doing just that, because in this case, the messenger is your paycheck.

Remaining oblivious to the true measurement of your effort isn't due only to trusting the information being provided; it's also used to fill a void of ignorance with something, anything. Applying some value to your activity is more reassuring than valueless empty space. But the untenable position of engaging in skepticism or complete ignorance is no basis of success for a Sales Professional. What you need is a Target.

CHAPTER 12

How Much Do I Have to Earn?

Prospecting Target Equations

THE PROSPECTING TARGET EQUATIONS provide a predetermined amount of hourly revenue that will be produced for a specific prospecting method. The equations will determine, at the outset of an activity, whether a required amount of revenue can be achieved. They will also provide a precalculated hourly revenue level that can be compared with a Target hourly revenue level. That goal can be a required quota amount, a commission amount, or any other earning potential desired. After the planned goal revenue is identified, it can be determined which method will get you there and the measurable difference between the two. The resulting metrics are used to monitor prospecting production and to compare the production with that of alternative methods.

Hourly Revenue Production Equation (HRP)

$$HRP = \left(\$X * \left(\frac{Appt}{HIT} * CR\right)\right)$$

Hourly Revenue Difference Equation (HRD)

$$HRD = \left(\$X * \left(\frac{Appt}{HIT} * CR\right)\right) - HRT$$

The Components of the Equations:

HRP	The Hourly Revenue Production
$X	The Average Dollar Revenue per Sale
Appt	One Appointment
HIT	The Hourly Time Needed to Gain One Appointment
CR	The Closing Ratio of the Prospecting Method
HRD	The Difference between the Hourly Revenue Production and the Hourly Target Revenue
HRT	The Hourly Revenue Target Goal Amount

Hourly Revenue Production Equation (HRP)

$$HRP = \left(\$X * \left(\frac{Appt}{HIT} * CR\right)\right)$$

The Hourly Revenue Production Equation is a tool used to quickly determine the revenue that will be produced in an hour of prospecting. In addition to providing immediate feedback, it obligates the Sales Professional to consistently gather the necessary production data associated with the individual selling situation. As Tactical Prospecting focuses on the hourly results of a prospecting method, Tactical Measurement quantifies the results in the same time period.

Using the data examples:

$X	$10,000
Appt	1
HIT	8
CR	10%

$$HRP = \left(\$10,000 * \left(\frac{1}{8} * 0.10\right)\right) = \$125$$

Hourly Revenue Difference Equation (HRD)

HRD = The Difference between the Hourly Revenue Production and the Hourly Target Revenue
$X = The Average Revenue Amount per Sale
Appt = One Appointment
HIT = The Hourly Time Needed to Gain One Appointment
CR = The Closing Ratio of the Prospecting Method
HRT = The Hourly Revenue Target Goal Amount

$$HRD = \left(\$X * \left(\frac{Appt}{HIT} * CR\right)\right) - HRT$$

The Hourly Revenue Difference Equation provides a measurement of the Target revenue level necessary to achieve a predetermined amount of production. After calculating the resulting hourly revenue, that value can be compared to a Targeted level. The solution will show whether the prospecting method produces more or less than the Target level. If the difference is below the Target level, then a simple calculation can be used to decide if an increase is needed in the prospecting success rate or sales closing ratio.

Again, using the previous data if the Target revenue production level is $100 per hour:

$X	$10,000
Appt	1
HIT	8
CR	10%
HRT	$100

$$HRD = \left(\$X * \left(\frac{Appt}{HIT} * CR\right)\right) - HRT$$

$$HRD = \left(\$10,000 * \left(\frac{1}{8} * 0.1\right)\right) - \$100$$

$$HRD = \left(\$10{,}000 * (0.125 * 0.1)\right) - \$100$$

$$HRD = (\$10{,}000 * 0.0125) - \$100$$

$$HRD = \$125 - \$100 = \$25$$

The solution shows that the difference between the actual production level and the Target level produces a production surplus of $25. In this case, the prospecting method is more than enough to achieve the goal. But what if the Target level is raised?

Assume that a goal for one month is $40,000, divided by the 173 hours.

$$\text{New Hourly Target} = \left(\frac{\$40{,}000}{173 \text{ hrs}}\right) = \$231$$

$$HRD = \left(\$X * \left(\frac{\text{Appt}}{\text{HIT}} * CR\right)\right) - HRT$$

$$HRD = \left(\$10{,}000 * \left(\frac{1}{8} * 0.1\right)\right) - \$231$$

$$HRD = \left(\$10{,}000 * (0.125 * 0.1)\right) - \$231$$

$$HRD = (\$10{,}000 * 0.0125) - \$231$$

$$HRD = \$125 - \$231 = -\$106$$

Now, the result shows a deficit of $106 per hour, and the prospecting method will not produce an adequate revenue volume to achieve the Target. Now what? Well, before an alternative method can be pursued, it should be determined what level of prospecting production is necessary to compensate for the difference, either in hours per appointment or closing ratio of each appointment.

Let's see what values we will need to determine the increase in the prospecting success rate:

$$HRD = (\$X * \left(\frac{Appt}{HIT} * CR\right)) - HRT$$

$$HRD = -\$106$$

Starting with the data, without a prospecting measurement (API) that is the new variable:

X = the variable or the required amount

$$\$10,000 * (X * 0.10) = -\$106$$

Now, multiply the average sales by the closing ratio:

$$\$10,000 * ((X) * 0.10) = -\$106$$

This leaves an amount of $1,000:

$$\$1,000 * (X) = -\$106$$

Divide both sides of the equation by the $1,000:

$$\frac{\$1,000 * (X)}{\$1,000} = \frac{-\$106}{\$1,000}$$

The prospecting variable difference equals -0.106:

$$(X) = -0.106$$

Since the HRD of -0.106 is a negative value, meaning a deficit, it must be added to the existing API to raise the needed Appointment Productivity Index. In theory, the opposite would be the case if there were a surplus value. However, it would be impractical to intentionally try to lower the appointment success index.

Add the new prospecting difference to the original prospecting index of 0.125:

$$0.106 + 0.125 = 0.231$$

Divide the one hour of prospecting time by the new Targeted prospecting-success index:

$$1 \text{ hour} / 0.231 = 4.32 \text{ hours}$$

The final calculation shows that a different prospecting method must produce 1 appointment for approximately every 4 hours of time. At the same closing ratio of 10 percent, this prospecting success level will compensate for the $106 deficit and produce the Target amount of $231 per hour. Now, the tactical thought process must be to determine which method will produce a single appointment in 4 hours as opposed to 8 hours. The simple question is, how do you double your prospecting productivity?

The importance isn't in asking if you should change the whole method or in asking if you should change the technique within the existing method; what's important is statistically accepting the need to change it, then looking for the answer.

Now that you've discovered the level of prospecting success necessary to achieve the Target, you must identify or create a prospecting method that achieves that level. Tactically speaking, find what method of prospecting will get you an appointment for 4 hours of work.

Alternatively, if instead of changing the prospecting method, increasing the closing ratio of those appointments is the focus, then you can determine what new closing ratio increase is needed.

$$HRD = \left(\$X * \left(\frac{Appt}{HIT} * CR \right) \right) - HRT$$

$$HRD = -\$106$$

Starting with the data, minus a prospecting measurement, which is the new variable:

$$\$10,000 * ((1/8) * X) = -\$106$$

Now, multiply the average sales by the prospecting index:

$$\$10,000 * 0.125 * (X) = -\$106$$

This leaves an amount of $1,250:

$$\$1,250 * (X) = -\$106$$

Divide both side of the equation by the $1,250:

$$\frac{\$1,250 * (X) = -\$106}{\$1,250 \qquad \$1,250}$$

This leaves the variable equal to -$106 divided by the $1,250:

$$(X) = \frac{-\$106}{\$1,250}$$

Again, since the HRD of -$106 is a negative value, meaning a deficit, and the resulting index value is also a negative, it must be added to the existing CR to raise the needed Closing Ratio. In theory, the opposite would be the case if there were a surplus value. However, it would be impractical to intentionally try to lower the existing Closing Ratio.

The prospecting variable difference equals -0.08:

$$(X) = -0.08$$

Since there's a deficit, add the new Closing-Ratio difference to the original closing ratio of 0.10:

$$0.10 + 0.08 = 0.18$$

The new closing ratio is 0.18 or 18 percent.

With the same prospecting success rate, the new closing rate must be 18 percent, an 80 percent increase in either the Sales Professional's negotiating ability or in the prospect quality, or both. Asking the right questions creates the roadmap to search for the correct answers. You can attempt to improve the closing potential by making the offer more attractive, changing the Targeted prospects, or any other positive manipulation of the deal structure. The key is searching for answers to the questions that never would have been asked without acquiring the necessary data in the first place.

The improvement—on the appointment-success side or the sales-closing side or a combination of the two—should be the focus of your tactical thought process. Determining what should be changed and how to change it is the invaluable result of first determining what level you're trying to reach and figuring out what numerical values are needed. But most important is that these variables and the tactics are determined at the outset, prior to aimlessly smiling and dialing.

So, at this point are you . . .

- Questioning your perceived revenue movement through time?
- Questioning the perceived value of your sales effort?
- Questioning the perceived measurement of your sales activity?

Well, it's not perceived. It's real—real movement, real effort, real activity.

Preventing Perdition

If you find yourself in prospecting purgatory, remember to avoid any future negatives by asking yourself these questions before engaging in a task . . .

How much will I earn?

How much am I being forced to earn?

How much do I have to earn?

. . . then calculate the answers by employing the appropriate Production Equations. There will be times when you're forced into these unearthly methods where the resulting metrics may be damned, but not necessarily eternal. Your talent must assume control and creatively alter the methods.

In one instance, I was forced to engage in the Hades of Prospecting Momentum Disruption, also known as the Territory Blitz. This activity consists of the entire salesforce traveling to one Sales Professional's territory to engage in cold calling by knocking on doors, as it were, of business offices, attempting to gain appointments. The appointments — or, in exceedingly rare potential instances, actual sales — would then be handed over to the Sales Professional who owned that territory. Then the following week, this activity is repeated with the entire salesforce in the second Sales Professional's territory, then the third territory in the third week, and so on.

Although for one week I had an entire sales team cold calling for me and would be handed any subsequent appointments they generated, I would have to travel to the other four territories in the following weeks and cold call for them. The metrics for the following four weeks would be a guaranteed **nothing**. *On the surface, this may sound like the ultimate version of sales philanthropy. Instead, it takes sales momentum and commits it to purgatory.*

In this example, there was a team of five Sales Professionals engaging in the activity for four hours. Adding in two hours for the round-trip commute to the territory, the event expended a total of six hours. To satisfy the requirements of the Territory Blitz task, I expended six hours, multiplied by five territories, for a total of thirty hours of Task Time. I was taking the poor production results of cold calling by itself, then further reducing its productivity index by doing it four more times for the benefit of others. Since this method is designed to forfeit any prospect opportunities that the Sales Professionals gained, I was guaranteed to generate an appointment production index of zero. Any productivity I could achieve from this method was completely dependent on what the other four Sales Professionals could generate when prospecting in my territory.

The resulting metrics for this task yielded the following results:

One appointment for 30 hours of investment of time with a closing ratio of 10 percent and average revenue of $10,000 per sale:

So, when I first asked, "How much do I have to earn?" I employed the Hourly Revenue Difference Equation and calculated $40,000 per month, which was my quota, or $231 per hour. And the following metrics were produced:

$X = $10,000
API = (1/30) = 0.033
SPI = 0.033 * 10% = 0.0033
HRP = $10,000 * 0.0033 = $33
HRT = $40,000 / 173 (hours in one month) = $231 per hour
HRD = $33 - $231 = -$198

With the monthly quota per hour as the Hourly Revenue Target and the Hourly Revenue Production of $33, the Territory Blitz provided a revenue index loss of $198 per hour.

Then when I asked, "How much am I being forced to earn?" and by substituting the Present Method Alliance Process for the New Method Territory Blitz, the unbearable answer was:

$X = $10,000
TT = 30 hours
New Method Territory Blitz
API = (1/30) = 0.033
SPI = 0.033 * (0.1) = 0.0033
Present Method Alliance Process
API = (1/.33) = 3
SPI = 3 * (0.65) = 1.95
CM = $10,000 * (0.0033- 1.95) * 30 = - $584,010

And when the Prospecting Revenue Momentum is visually expressed in the following chart . . .

Prospecting Method Revenue Momentum

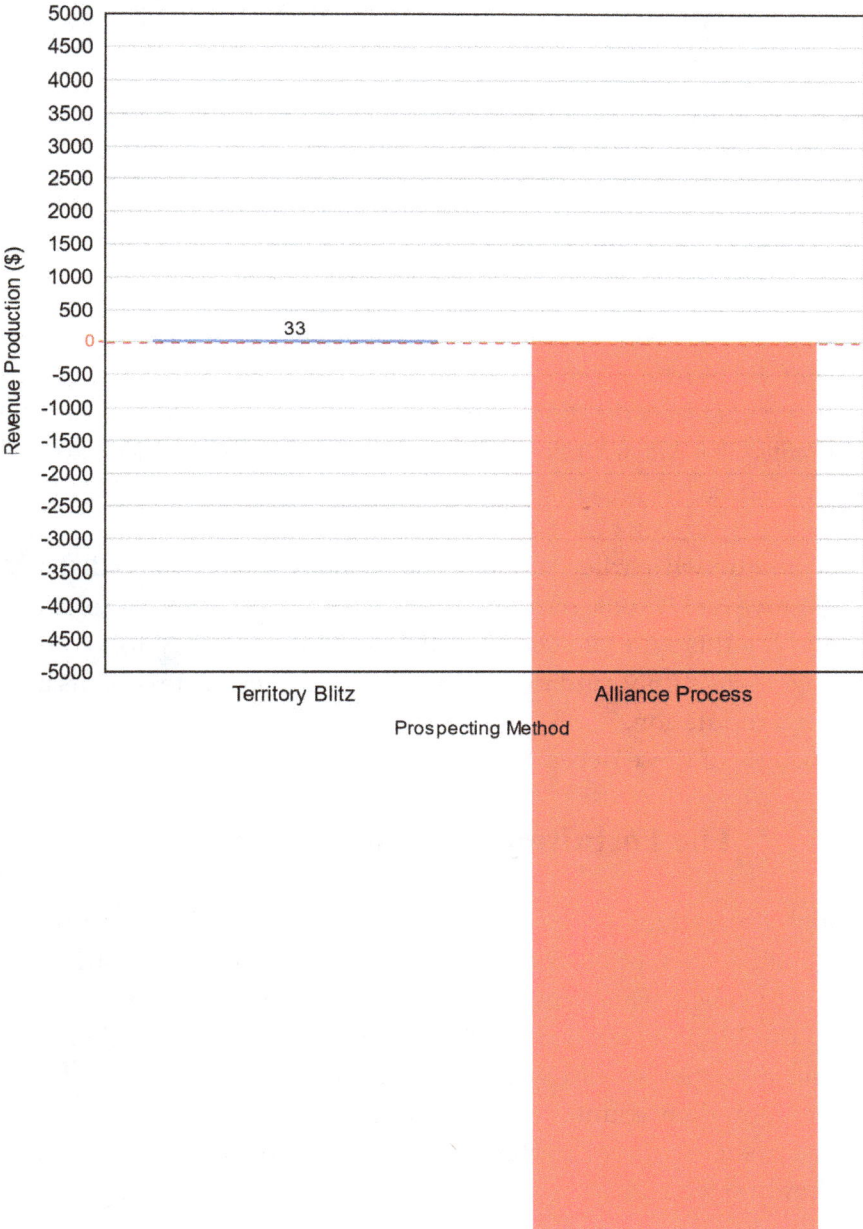

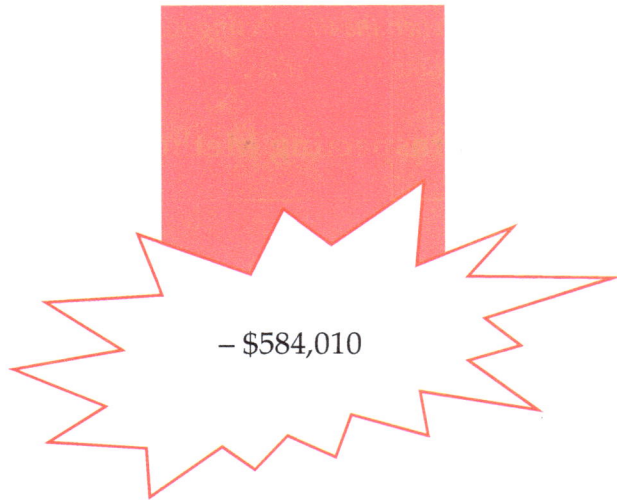

$$- \$584,010$$

It's off the charts.

*By changing from the Alliance Process to the Territory Blitz Method, the Comparison Momentum resulted in an infernal **negative** $584,010 revenue index.*

As mentioned earlier, there were creative ways to avoid the task; however, it took more cunning than talent. And, unfortunately, it's this type of scheming that's often necessary to avoid Management's folly, and undeservedly earn Sales Professionals a crooked reputation.

A couple of these deceptive devices include:

The Fortuitous Fishbowl Method

Sales Professionals are required to return from the Territory Blitz with a stack of business cards, presumably from the offices they cold called. This provided supervisors with proof that they really did Blitz the territory and didn't merely pretend to. To get around this, they would visit any local diner, which often had a fishbowl on their counter full of business cards deposited by patrons for some type of contest giveaway. If a business card was randomly selected by the diner, that business would win a prize, like a free lunch. The remaining cards were used as names to be contacted for marketing purposes to promote additional business. To employ the Fortuitous Fishbowl Method, two Sales Professionals would have lunch there, and while one paid the bill, the other would sneak their hand into the fishbowl and steal all the cards. These business cards were then turned in to the supervisor as proof. In the time it took to eat lunch, they satisfied the Blitz verification process and had a good meal.

The Sidestep-Siesta Method

The title pretty much explains it all. This method of avoiding the Territory Blitz consists of driving to a quiet, inconspicuous area of a parking lot and taking a nap. There are, however, two specific requirements to perform this avoidance task. The first is that the Sales Professional must have a sufficient number of business cards saved up from their previous years in the profession to submit for verification. And the second is that these cards must have addresses that match the territory being canvassed. Oh wait, there's a third requirement: you must be a supervisor because they're usually the only ones using this method.

It's Time

It's time to view your productivity as a function of your talent and a function of your effort. The Alliance Analytics measurement tools are the means to gain control over these functions. The next time you're about to take on a new position—or are forced to attend a meeting, institute a new prospecting method, or perform a mandatory IT procedure—ask yourself: how much will I earn, how much am I being forced to earn, and how much do I have to earn? Then calculate the answers.

PART FIVE

Time's Up!

I HAVE PRESENTED A blueprint for prospecting success that is so greatly needed in the sales profession that without it, the modern-day Sales Professional is destined for the high turnover servitude of Management's prospecting control. Now, I have concentrated on the power of the Alliance Process for illustrative purposes and have drawn comparisons to other forms of prospecting.

There may be a place in the prospecting repertoire for other types of appointment-generating techniques. If so, the key difference is how it relates to the proportional time invested in each. The least amount of your time should be spent performing the activity with the lowest success percentage, and the most amount of your time spent with the highest. However, the opposite occurs, and worse, is often required.

What about the competition as it relates to these prospecting activities that produce miserable results? If competitors are also using the same prospecting methods, then who has the advantage? Who would get the appointment and why would they get it? Are they better telemarketers or door knockers? The "appointment-getter" usually has some inherent advantage, be it an existing satisfied customer, a more familiar brand name, or the ability to offer the lowest price. A market is filled with dozens of salespeople obediently performing the same rotten techniques directed at the same organizations, believing that perseverance alone will win the appointment. And whoever is left standing gains Management's praise and a real chance to succeed by being fed the qualified prospects.

Finally, it's important to understand that "always prospecting" isn't the same as "always identifying Opportunity." If I merely conduct a trial-and-error request for an appointment—even if it is isolated to the proper customer—it's still just a low-odds gamble in which you need to be lucky and hope the activity has been timed well with the need. That strategy is too dangerous to base your compensation on, let alone an entire profession.

CHAPTER 13

Where Are Those Complaints Now?

NOW THAT YOU'VE RECEIVED an in-depth tutorial on Tactical Prospecting and the Alliance Prospecting Process, do the typical sales obstacles we reviewed at the beginning really have any significance in the new prospecting world? Look at them one more time and ask yourself, after becoming proficient at the Alliance Process, will I ever have to overcome these obstacles again?

So, when . . .

I can't get by the gatekeeper—There is no longer a gate.

So, when . . .

They said our price is too high—Price, or perceived price, is no longer an obstacle to gain the appointment; it is now part of the negotiation.

So, when . . .

Nobody knows us—They know you ahead of time.

So, when . . .

The economy is slow—The prospects with purchasing intent are isolated for you.

So, when . . .

I don't have my business cards yet—Really? Do I even have to discuss this one?

These are the sales burdens you may still hear from the less proficient, but you will never have to utter them again yourself.

Sales Trainers' Advice

To illustrate how experientially destitute sales-prospecting training can be, I've listed a few of the most ridiculous sales trainer answers to questions about prospecting asked by sales trainees. Keep in mind, I've heard these exchanges with my very own ears:

1. **Trainee:** *How can I make more appointments on the phone?*
   Trainer: *Just make more calls. You don't have to learn or get better at anything. It takes no more thought than picking up the phone more often.* (So, I spent tens of thousands of dollars and years of effort on a college education to be told that my professional position doesn't require any learning, thought, or need to get better?)

2. **Trainee:** *Are there any new methods we can use to increase our success rate?*
   Trainer: *There are no shortcuts; prospecting is a necessary evil.*

I'm sorry, I have to say something about this one. Prospecting is not a necessary evil. It is the nuts-and-bolts activity of your profession and the most important activity for success in sales— more than negotiating, overcoming objections, and updating your CRM notes. It takes intelligence, effort, discipline, and most importantly, creativity. These attributes are usually called talent. This answer offered by the sales trainer demonstrates the systemic lack of understanding. Prospecting isn't a necessary evil; it's a necessary ability.

3. **Trainee:** *What can I do when I encounter "No Soliciting" signs?*
   Trainer: *Have a contest with the sales team to see who can pry off from the doors the most "No Soliciting" signs and bring them back to the office.*

4. **Trainee:** *How can I improve my role-playing?*
   Trainer: *I'll create a homework assignment with a pretend company, and you can practice at home.*

5. **Trainee:** *What is the best way to network?*
   Trainer: *I don't teach networking.*

Allies Sales Trainer Answers

If these questions were asked after learning the Alliance Process, and if I have done my job by fulfilling my obligation to you, there should only be one answer to all these questions:

1. **Trainee:** *How can I make more appointments on the phone?*
   Trainer: *Call Allies.*

2. **Trainee:** *Are there any new methods we can use to increase our success rate?*
   Trainer: *The Alliance Process.*

3. **Trainee:** *What can I do when I encounter "No Soliciting" signs?*
   Trainer: *Visit Allies.*

4. **Trainee:** *How can I improve my role-playing?*
   Trainer: *There's no pretending with Allies.*

5. **Trainee:** *What is the best way to network?*
   Trainer: *Hunt for Allies.*

Revisit Some of The Basics

IT Prospecting Tools

I was hesitant about offering a section on the multitude of software-based tools too early in the book. They're prevalent and could be used in Tactical Prospecting but, too often, tools are expected to accomplish the task that they're designed only to assist. Everyone is looking for the magic bullet that will improve their present sales situation and somehow do the work for them. This belief is by no means the direct fault of the Sales Professional. The problem is that the basic tenets of Tactical Prospecting aren't understood, subsequently aren't taught, and are very often discouraged by Management. Without an initial foundation, tools are given more power than they deserve. And as with most tools, if they are not implemented with a knowledge, an understanding, and most importantly, a goal, then they are merely useless implements waiting for a master. I settled on placing this section at the end of the book so that, first, the methodology could be completely absorbed. If by now you have come to understand and believe in the Alliance Process, then there is no need to look for ancillary tools, as you will discover them for yourself. And with the myriad of software databases and internet-based communications as basic as email and as powerful as video conferencing, Tactical Prospecting has even greater potential. However, always remember that technology tools are just tools; they will not prospect for you.

The Networking Event

Hunt, Don't Mingle

With an understanding of the elements of Tactical Prospecting, the Alliance Process, and its associated devices, I must address the coveted *Networking Event* as it relates to Mindset Identification. To truly succeed when attending an event designed to facilitate interaction with a variety of people, there should be a tactical plan in place with the single objective of gaining a new Ally. There may be a hundred chances

> **The Mindset is defined as possessing the ability to perform these tasks:**
> **1.** The ability to identify an Opportunity.
> **2.** The ability to engage an Opportunity.
> **3.** The ability to negotiate an Opportunity

to have discussions about everything under the sun, spend thousands of dollars, and walk away with business cards, T-shirts, and stress balls. That is not a plan and certainly not a productive objective. When encountering others in this setting, the objective of any conversation is to determine as quickly as possible if the individual has a Business-Development Mindset and then plan a follow-up interaction. And the number of potential Allies isn't at all proportional to the size of the event. In my experience, the bigger the event, the worse the networking Opportunity, because larger events create a greater distraction from identifying the qualified Allies. This compounds the waste because the larger events are typically more expensive, so valuable time and dollars are expended with a lower return. If you can come away from an event with a single Ally, then it is a success, because they will be a long-term provider of Leads.

However, trade events are different because that type of interaction is designed to promote products and must be viewed purely for its sales results. But has anyone ever gone to a Chamber of Commerce social event with the intention of buying something? I've observed that the longer participants converse together in a group, the less the discussion is about developing any business. Quite often these interactions are used as a social lifeboat, until the participants feel comfortable enough in the sea of event-goers to float off to the next lifeboat of minglers.

A Planned Event

Preparatory planning will depend on the theme of a specific event, and you should conduct a review of the organizations and the individual participants. This will in no way provide any insight into their individual Mindset, nor will it determine for you who is and isn't a qualified Ally; it is merely a guide or a warm-up for you to get your Tactical Prospecting processes in gear. The proper Targets derived from this initial analysis are the ones that are accessible to these participants. The plan is to identify the people with access to your Targets, make them Contacts by engaging in a Significant Interaction, and if they are qualified, create an Ally.

The second step is to initiate conversations with the participants as quickly as possible to ascertain their Target customer, then **Anchor Seed**. If the **Counterweighing** behavior is not engaged by them in terms of both interest in your Lead and offering a Lead in return, then discard the Contact and move on.

Anchor Seed: offering Leads to an Ally first, before receiving Leads.

Counterweigh: gaining Leads from an Ally in return for providing Leads first.

CHAPTER 14

The Museum of Radical Prospecting

Radical Allies

ONCE IMPLEMENTING THE nuts-and-bolts tactics of the Alliance Process, it in no way should become so mechanical that the process inhibits sales creativity. I've found that in all aspects of selling, what is considered radical creativity today becomes a new process, a new market, or a new vertical that was never thought of before.

Transient Process Ally to a Permanent Process Ally to a POS Ally

The Chauffeuring Method

When I was an entry-level Sales Professional in a major city, I was attempting to gain an appointment with the owner of a limousine company who had an office in the lobby of a hotel. Due to a series of scheduling mishaps on both his and my part, the appointment kept getting canceled. Although the snafus were mutual, I received the brunt of the blame.

Finally, he was fed up with the interactions and refused to take my calls. I realized the potential sales volume that could be generated from this account, not only by my supplying a product to his employees but also by his reselling the product to his customers. The opportunity was too great. I couldn't give it up, so I needed a unique way to regain his trust and gain an appointment.

As I said, he controlled every aspect of his business, including the dispatching of the drivers, so I knew that he would be communicating with them over their two-way radios. I took a chance and ordered a car from his limo service to bring me to that very same hotel. I was willing to

*"**bust in**" on him for one last try. It was worth the risk. Maybe he would feel gratitude that I paid for his service and would*

Bust In: an unannounced follow-up visit to a prospect.

re-engage the appointment. Although, paying for his service was in no way thought of as a means of regaining rapport.

The driver picked me up, and we started toward the hotel. Then, surprisingly, he radioed to the driver to confirm the pickup, and that was my chance to pounce. The driver grabbed the mic to respond. I quickly told the driver that he was a friend of mine and I wanted to say hello. I reached way over the seat through the space in the sliding plexiglass opening. He handed me the mic, and I reintroduced myself. He responded, "Oh, it's you." I ignored that and pitched him the whole deal over the radio. I'm not sure, but I seem to remember after every counteroffer, we kept saying, "over."

He was a Transient Process Ally until I sold the account, then he became a Permanent Process Ally. Then, after a bit of time, I structured a reseller deal so that he could lease our product to his customers on a day-by-day basis. He gained additional revenue for himself while virtually paying the cost of the products used by his company. At that point, he became a POS Reseller Ally.

Transient Process Ally to a Partner Ally

The Job-Interview Method

An extreme radical technique of bypassing the gatekeeper and the rest of those prospecting obstacles is to apply for a job with a Target. That's right; apply for a job! Now, I know this would be frowned upon by your supervisor, even if they did understand the objective. And in all fairness, the reason is obvious. You may get hired. However, the probability objective isn't designed to weigh in favor of that, although there is more than a slight chance. I've calculated 90:10 against because the thought process in the meeting is more sales-oriented than employment-oriented. The primary objective is to identify a person with access and to establish any type of Ally. Therefore, the notion that you may be the right person for the job will be diminished because of the poor matching. If you are hunting for a complementary set of industry characteristics and they're not a perfect match with your present industry, that can weigh against you as an employee candidate. Or the pay scale may not match your experience level and that can weigh against you as well. "Weigh against you" means, as a job candidate, it strengthens you as a potential Ally with the interviewer.

The key is to interview with a Contact that has the proper ranking and Mindset. The key isn't just gaining an interview; the key is gaining a meeting with the proper Contact in the form of an interview. There won't be a 90:10 ratio if the interview is with the first-level human resources person. If you plan on interviewing with an HR-type hiring entity, you might as well ask to meet the gatekeeper instead. That would have a better chance of success.

If there isn't a quality match for you as a hire, but you've established a quality match in terms of rapport, then a future Ally relationship is almost inevitable. And who knows, maybe there will be a quality match as a candidate, and you're given an offer of employment even though that wasn't your initial intention. Remember, that's the serendipity that benefits you and your financial success — the reason you're reading this thing in the first place.

After beginning a consulting position, I then applied for a sales position with a computer-networking company to meet the sales director and attempt to establish a POS Partner (at least initially) to sell the product to his client base. Next would be to establish a Lead-exchange mechanism for the same type of customers, as well as the other Contacts he had. He was a very amiable person who understood my selling abilities but realized that I couldn't earn as much as I needed. So, he didn't want to take the turnover chance by hiring me. Completely expected. However, I knew he had the Mindset, so I followed up with him a week later, describing my sales-consulting position, the product I was selling, and requested a meeting to discuss Opportunities. The rest you probably know by now.

Although this was a pleasant success, there are also nightmare scenarios because some interviewers not only don't have any Business-Development Mindset but also have no interviewing Mindset either. When this perfect storm of inability occurs, you can become trapped in a room with a "peel back the onion," Pleonastic Ally, trying to trip you up by asking a redundant, never-ending series of identical probing questions simply phrased differently, until the imaginary onion creates real tears.

One time, I was being tortured in an interview by this onion-peeler who spent the whole time trying to catch me in a non-existent lie by asking one question about twenty different ways. He was disagreeing with my answers to open-ended questions, as if he was trying to disprove my favorite color. I was trapped.

Then, he abruptly demanded, "Let's get serious. Let's say I drove to your house, went into your personal library, reached on the shelf for your autobiography, opened the book to the chapter called "Success." What does it say?"

At first, I reached into the recesses of my sarcasm library. The only reason I ever reach that point is that when an interviewer asks such a question, they have no intention of hiring you. But then I decided that reality would be the wittiest response.

"It doesn't say *anything," I exclaimed. "It's a picture book. There's a picture of my thousand-dollar watch, my brand-new sports car, my million-dollar house." Then I asked, "What does yours say, 'Avoid threatening your own job by not hiring guys like me?'" Which he avoided.*

Transient Process Ally to Passive Ally

The Landlord Method

I purchased residential real estate several years ago, mainly as an investment. The type of property, size, location, and cost were based on the appreciation potential and ease of attracting higher-end tenants. But I also considered the Opportunity to gain access to the tenants' Targets. First, I identified the Target organizations, then I purchased properties that would match those Targets in terms of location and property type. Then I marketed the homes to those organizations. Although this method was designed with Tactical Prospecting as the secondary objective, it was nevertheless a business-development Opportunity that should be viewed as a means of gaining ancillary productive serendipities. So, to market it, I communicated with the human-resource departments of corresponding Target organizations who typically handle relocation. I followed up using internet real-estate ads and emailing the rental information to these organizations. In this manner, I was able to create high-access-ranking Passive Allies.

Some of the Passive Allies included two presidents of a multi-national corporation, a regional VP in logistics, the CIO of an airline, a small-business owner with tremendous POS Reseller potential, a VP of a multinational construction company, an operations manager of a national food distributor, and a CEO of a software-development company, not to mention the high-access-ranking professionals that I met who were simply viewing the property. I've done business with several of these entities in addition to creating several Passive Allies to be accessed later.

While one of the CEOs of a multinational was living in my rental home, I was restricted by my own company from making a sales appointment with his organization because of some of the silly reasons I have explained throughout the book. He was a kind person who appreciated my assistance with his family since he traveled quite often. They were foreigners left alone in unfamiliar surroundings. So, when he was relocated back to his home country, we took a picture together with his arm around me out of gratitude.

Back to reality and the CRM database, Management was in control of this prospect and had notes stating that they were "running out of ways" to try to get an appointment with the organization and may have to delete the prospect from the database. Because, to Management, the importance of keeping the CRM database happy can't be understated! Anyway, I uploaded the picture to the CRM account and wrote, "Before you delete this prospect, maybe I can help." The response was to refrain from pursuing prospects not assigned to me. I was able to establish an appointment for the favored senior sales representative whose name was unfairly stuck onto the prospect in the CRM.

Now, these are examples of creative Tactical Prospecting that I admit are a bit radical. But, as I hope you can see, they are designed with the principles of Allies at their core, as well as talent. More as a warning than a guideline step, individual Allies are not interchangeable between you and your colleagues. They are unique to you and possess their specific characteristics as a function of the relationship they have with you alone. With Allies, there appears to be an immediate loyalty formed with the first sales "being" with whom they form a business-development relationship. This relationship can never be expected to have the same productivity value if transferred to others.

Some "being," not human, is email-marketing software that is designed to project a human identity. They are given a name, their own email address and the prospecting message has friendly, personalized wording that convince the recipient that they originated from a real human being. The program is designed to generate leads which are given to real human Sales Professionals to manage from that point.

In one case, I received a lead from a marketing service that used Artificial Intelligence software to generate appointments. When I contacted the individual prospect, he declared his loyalty to the AI generated identity that he believed to be a real person and refused to work with me. He said he had a good working relationship with that "person" so far. I couldn't tell the prospect the truth and risk humiliating him. So, I explained that I manage the appointments after they are initially created by that "person." But, he accused me of poaching and wouldn't take my calls after multiple attempts.

Why Allies bond with the initial entity who created the relationship and no one else can probably never sufficiently be explained. And, in the world of Tactical Prospecting, it never needs to be explained.

CONCLUSION

It's Time to Start Over

The Penultimate Performance

I was in a meeting with a VP of sales discussing a potential consulting position. While having a seemingly intelligent discussion on my prospecting methods, he abruptly stopped the conversation to see my methods in action. He reached his arm across the desk and demanded, "Sell me this pen!" I realized that he hadn't absorbed a single thing I said.

So, I took the pen from his hand, paused for a moment, and confidently responded, "I don't have to sell it to you. By prospecting my way, you'll invite me here to buy it."

After that happened, I began writing this book with that very same pen.

The Sales Professional's Survival Guide Pocket Reference

Since time is my guide, and I greatly respect yours, here are the bare-bones procedural tactics used to engage the Alliance Process.

1. Never, never, never let emotion decide the quality or category of an Ally. Even if you expected more production from an Ally, recategorize them. In the proper category, they will produce what's expected.

2. Use the analytic equations to determine a benchmark index of your prospecting.

3. Make a chart with inverted funnel columns representing each Ally Category.

4. Review your inventory of Contacts, whether friends, colleagues, coworkers, or any other individual with whom you have had any Significant Interaction in your life, regardless of the length of time since your last interaction, and communicate with them.

5. Once an agreed-upon relationship is created, list these new Allies in each column according to their characteristic Mindset. Remember, they can and will change categories after further interactions. The Process Ally column will be disproportionately longer than the other columns due to the larger number of Contacts met during the business dealings that possess the Mindset.

6. Establish a commitment level of new Allies to be gained in a specified time period. Yes, a quota, but place it on yourself. Don't let others do it for you, because then it will probably be an unrealistic number that they would never place on themselves.

7. Interact with the Allies and gather information.

8. Move to equally balance the category lists by forming new interactions with new Contacts that are offered to you.

9. Meet with the Contacts and exchange Target information.

10. Never, never, never feel compelled to revert to cold-calling organizations for your appointments merely because these organizations match your Target customer. If the Allies you have are not producing, recategorize them and get new ones. However, if you happen to be standing next to an office that looks like a Target match for whatever reason, then cold call it. What the heck, you're there anyway. Just don't go randomly visit a hundred of them, using up your whole day, to feel satisfied. Management will feel that for you.

ALLIES CATEGORIZATION POCKET REFERENCE

To quickly determine the categories that best fit your Allies, you can start by asking yourself a series of guideline questions. These questions are an informal technique used as a precursor to both the more-advanced Categorization Equation Tool and the most advanced, intuition.

For an immediate determination of the proper category after you've identified a Lead, have had a Significant Interaction and made them a Contact, and then created an agreed-upon relationship forming an Ally, research their database of people for potential Targets. Then ask yourself:

1. Does this Ally have access to Targets? If yes, place them in one of the five categories: Passive, Process, Partner, Party, or POS.

2. Will this Ally provide Leads without me asking? If yes, then move them into one of the top-three producing categories: Partner, Party, or POS.

3. Does this Ally run a business? If yes, then move them into one of the top two categories: Party or POS Ally.

4. Does this Ally presently resell your industry products or a complementary product? If yes, then move them in the top category: POS Ally.

These are the basic questions that will provide a perfunctory analysis to get you started. As you become more proficient with the identification process, it will become more intuitive and second nature based on your experience with the Ally's past behaviors, until the proficiency can reach the level of intuition.

ALLIANCE ANALYTICS POCKET REFERENCE

1. How much will I earn?

Monthly Prospecting Production Equation

$$\dfrac{\left((\text{TPH-NPH}) - \left(\text{NCSAppt} * \text{NCSApptH}\right) * \left(\frac{\text{AveV}}{\text{MSC}}\right) - \left(\text{ECSAppt} * \text{ECSApptH} * \left(\frac{\text{AveV}}{\text{MSC}}\right)\right)\right)}{\left(\text{HPAppt} + \text{NCSApptH} + \left(\text{NCSApptH} * \frac{(\text{AveV}-1)}{\text{MSC}}\right)\right)} * \left(\left(\text{ARS} * \text{NCCR}\right) + \left(\text{ARS} * \text{ECSAppt} * \text{ECCR}\right)\right) * \frac{(\text{MSC}+1)}{2}$$

- Total Available Prospecting Hours per Month
- Total Revenue per Closing Ratio
- Sales Cycle Factor
- Total Hours to Gain One Appointment
- Months to Close a Sale
- MSC

The Appointment Productivity Index

$$\text{API} = \frac{\text{Appointment Gained}}{\text{Hourly Investment of Time}}$$

The Sales Productivity Index

$$\text{SPI} = \left(\frac{\text{Appointment Gained}}{\text{Hourly Investment of Time}}\right) * \text{Closing Ratio}$$

The Appointment Productivity Cost

$$APC = \dfrac{\text{Hourly Dollar Rate}}{\left(\dfrac{\text{Appointment Gained}}{\text{Hourly Investment of Time}}\right)}$$

The Sales Productivity Cost

$$SPC = \dfrac{\text{Hourly Dollar Rate}}{\left(\dfrac{\text{Appointment Gained}}{\text{Hourly Investment of Time}} * \text{Closing Ratio}\right)}$$

2. How much am I being forced to earn?

The Prospecting Momentum Equation

$$PM = \$X * \left(\dfrac{\text{Appt}}{\text{HIT}} * CR\right) * TT$$

The Target Momentum Difference Equation

$$TMD = PM - (HRT * TT)$$

The Comparison Momentum Equation

New Task   Existing Task

$$CM = \$X * \left(\left(\dfrac{\text{Appt}}{\text{HIT}} * CR\right) - \left(\dfrac{\text{Appt}}{\text{HIT}} * CR\right)\right) * TT$$

3. How much do I have to earn?

Hourly Revenue Production Equation (HRP)

$$HRP = \left(\$X * \left(\frac{Appt}{HIT} * CR\right)\right)$$

Hourly Revenue Difference Equation (HRD)

$$HRD = \left(\$X * \left(\frac{Appt}{HIT} * CR\right)\right) - HRT$$

ABOUT THE AUTHOR

Mike LaRusso is a forty-year sales veteran working in diverse sales roles for a multitude of organizations. As an independent sales contractor, consultant, analyst, and writer, he leverages critical thinking, analytics and sales creativity, providing organizations with prospecting methods designed for new business development.

www.ingramcontent.com/pod-product-compliance
Lightning Source LLC
Chambersburg PA
CBHW071554210326
41597CB00019B/3234